I0101983

Juliet's Love

By T.A. Starks

Young Romero left the hard streets of Chicago to pursue his dream of becoming a published author, but on the streets of Long Beach, California, he encounters a young white runaway by the name of Juliet. After saving Juliet's life in a filthy alleyway, the two began to form an unbreakable bond and formulate a master plan to get paid major bread. Once his team of females starts pulling in cold, hard-earned cash and bowing to him as king, that's when problems start to arrive one after another. Money, sex, murder, and more sex follow Romero and his loyal trio of females as they do their best to get rich and stay rich as a team on the deadly streets of Long Beach, California.

Dedicated to everyone that believed in me, and my craft.

Chapter 1

She was disgusted by him. Seeing his out-of-shape, deadbeat body lying on the living room sofa, drunk, she hated him and wanted to smash the half-drunken bottle of Jack over his head. The stink of him made her want to vomit as unwanted thoughts ran through her mind of her own father forcing himself on her.

Night after night ever since she was nine years old he would enter her room and do sexual acts to and on her. He called it love but she knew it wasn't; her father was a rotten pig who twisted his only child's view of love into something bogus. Juliet didn't understand why she never told anyone about the things her father was doing, but she could only figure it was fear. Fear of the "system," fear of being separated from the only family she really ever had.

Her mother had passed away when she was fourteen and she was left alone with her dad. At first things were bearable as far as the household routine went. "Daddy dearest" would come home late from work, crawl into Juliet's bed, do his thing and be done. He'd give her thirty or forty bucks—like hush money—she'd go to school and stay out late every night just to be alone. But lately… things had gotten worse, bad, and violent. Plus she was at the age where what was going on was all too clear as to being wrong. Her dad would come home drunk from drinking at the local pub he'd come into her room and violently force himself on her.

Juliet would protest with verbal no's and stops but that would only bring on the choking and the slapping. Why was she cursed to live such a life? Why was she chosen?

She couldn't take it anymore. She was about to make her great escape. So, in the late night hours she packed her bags, pocketed her summer savings of $450 and headed for the back door. Juliet crept silently through the hallway and as she did she could hear the light snores from her father and the TV playing. Once in the kitchens he took a box of Pop-Tarts and went for the back door. She never wanted to see that house again. She never wanted to see the streets of Boise again, and if she ever saw her scumbag of a father again it would be too soon. Out into the night she went, heading for the bus station with new eyes and new hope for the future.

*   *   *

"Bill! I had plans tonight. That's not fair!" Sandra yelled with disappointment.

"Yeah, well, plans change and life's not always fair. Don't leave this house, and I mean that, and you call me Dad or Daddy or Father, no more of this 'Bill' crap. I'll be home around eleven." Sandra's father left out the front door and the loud slam of the door made her cringe. Overwhelmed with emotions she burst into tears running down the hallway to her room.

She slammed her door, diving onto her bed. She hated this. She hated her mother for being a drunken bitch who forced her to live with her step-father. Over the last few years, life was pure hell. Sandra would fight verbally with her mother about dumb things. The arguments would lead to a physical altercation where Sandra would end up losing. Every since the divorce of her parents, things were bad. Back and forth in court battling it out about who gets the kid, about who was the more fit parent. In the end her mother just gave up and told the judge she was ready to hand over full custody.

Life wasn't pleasant with her drunken mother and it sure wasn't with her power struck step-father who felt like he was "top shit" because he owned a tire store, drove an old 2001 BMW, and had a nice-sized house. Bert, her step-father, really didn't want her around because it messed up his bachelor vibe with the local groupies.

God... she wished her real dad were still alive. He'd take her away from all this and life would be worth living again. It was a Friday night and Sandra had made plans to go skating with her girlfriends downtown. Now she couldn't go, yet again. This was not the life she wanted. She had dreams that required being out of the house, on center stage, and traveling the free world. It was time to leave. So in her anger she started to pack her bags.

She gathered up key pieces of clothing and also her life's savings of only $1,500. She had to go someplace far away. Someplace where she could shine and pursue her lifelong dream of becoming an international model. So once she was done packing she called the south-end bus station and booked a seat to the West Coast. It was "goodbye" to little old Maine, and "hello" to the Golden State of California.

* * *

Long Beach, California, the land of endless opportunity, state of stars and the mighty lookers. Pure sunshine almost all the time and thousands of beautiful women half naked tanning at the beaches. The West Coast was the new home for Midwest, up-and-coming Romero Hinton. Having been on the road for what seemed like weeks he had finally arrived. Equipped with only two duffel bags and his laptop backpack, $2500 and a dream… he was ready to become the next big-time somebody.

Romero had come from the Westside of Chicago by Greyhound bus. He had somehow managed to be the first person since his dead Uncle Charles to graduate high school and go on to Malcolm X Community College. It wasn't easy growing up in one of the country's most dangerous cities, he had to guard his chest and watch his back 24/7 from all the city's gangs.

Romero really never thought that he would amount to anything, but when he kept earning A's in all his writing classes and English classes, and D's in all the rest of his classes, well… someone who cared took notice. So one of his teachers began to enter him into small writing contests and he would win. Next he'd be entered into a slightly more advanced contest and he would also win that. By the end of high school, Romero had won over sixteen writing contests and was offered an anonymous two-year funding to the community college of his choice.

Romero was honored to receive the gift and went to school, but the higher field of education was way harder than high school. He could ditch school without detention but his grades would fall. He could slack on homework and get no calls of concern from his teachers, but his grades would fall because he would fail tests. Not to mention he was still semi living the street life. He would some days pick up a "G-pack" and sling rock cocaine with his guys, or stupidly go on a ride-along with his boys and witness a drive-by shooting.

Romero was drowning and he wanted more out of life. He knew that with his talent in writing plays, novels, short stories, screenplays, and novellas, he could be the next big African American author. So, just like that he dropped all his classes, packed a couple of bags, took his savings, told his mama, "I'll see you soon," and headed west. Stepping off the bus, Romero took his first deep breath of West Coast air. He smiled brightly with squinted eyes as he made his way down the station's platform to a fleet of parked cabs. He approached one and spoke to the man from the sidewalk into the passenger side window.

"Excuse me, but is you in service?" he asked, squinting. The heat from the sunrays baked his brown neck, it had to be every bit of 80-85 degrees and Romero regretted wearing black jeans.

"Sure, I'm in service, where you need to go?" the thin cabby asked, folding up his newspaper and tossing it next to him.

"Uh... Can you take me to a real cheap motel?"

"Cheap motel? Hop on in and let's see what we can find ya." The cabby drove through long beach and Romero took in the sights. "Cali" was just like on TV, it was all palm trees, beaches, and blondes. It was nothing like Chicago, he thought, but once the cabby made a few detours the land looked just like home. Suddenly the trees were gone and the streets were littered with trash. On just about each corner was a liquor store or vacant lot which looked like a landfill. Whores and hobos walked the blocks and there was gang graffiti all over buildings. Suddenly Romero felt like he had never left the Westside. After a bogus ride in what seemed like an attempt to burn the cab meter the taxi pulled into the lot of a place called Lucky Nights Inn. The sign out front read: "Nice rooms for the best price - $45 a night." When the cabby was paid he entered the motel and was greeted by a small Asian woman. The front desk area was cooled with central air conditioning and it felt good on his moist skin.

"Can I help you?" the elderly Asian woman said. Romero thought she would speak with broken English but she spoke very well.

"Yeah, I was wondering did y'all have any type of extended-stay deals?"

"Yes we do. If you stay for four days or more you get a $45 discount. Will you be staying for more than four days?" she asked, smiling.

"Uh... yeah, I wanna stay for like a month. How much is that?" The clerk began to do the math on her computer and told him.

"That would be $1,080, but since you rent for a month you get the deposit fee back which is $80, so, you're actually only paying $1,000."

Romero wasn't thrilled with coming off a grand his first day in California, but he had to lodge someplace. So he paid the clerk and was handed his key to his room. His room was located in the back of the motel on the second floor. The Lucky Nights Inn wasn't an in-house motel but an out-house motel where all the room doors were located facing the open area. Romero didn't care for that part but he had no choice. When he came into his room, he found it to be average and nice enough. Just like most motels there was a queen-size bed, nightstand, dresser, card table, and a twenty-inch mounted flat screen TV on the wall. He closed the door behind him and locked it. He instantly turned on the air conditioner and tossed his bags on the floor and table. He sat on the bed and bounced up and down testing it for softness. Then he sat in silence nodding his head looking around the small room.

"Home sweet home," he said out loud. Romero then got this laptop out, plugged it in and let it boot up. While it did he decided to take a hot shower before getting to work.

*   *   *

Young Juliet Witmore had only been in the Golden State three days and she already felt lost. On her first days she enjoyed the freedom of not being bound and took in all the sights of the large city. She made her way down to the beach where hundreds of people tanned, played volleyball, swam, and had a good time. Juliet was on cloud nine as she submerged her feet into the warm sands and splashed around in the Pacific Ocean. She also strolled the boardwalk where she window-shopped and ate tasty vendor foods.

She had resided at a Motel-8 and ordered pizza, took a soothing bath, and watched cable all night. The days next she made her way to the city's mall. She only intended to do a bit more window-shopping but she let temptation get the best of her and she bought a few cheap bathing suits, Nike cross-trainer shoes, and sunglasses. This was the life, she thought as she sipped on a soda in the mall food court.

Juliet's funds had diminished before she knew it. By day four she only had enough cash to feed herself, she didn't even have the means to rent another room for a night. Now the sun was going down and the night was almost upon the city. She didn't know what to do. So, for a long time she sat in a Mickey D's until it closed, then when she had no choice but to leave she walked aimlessly through the city. Finally she thought about the beach and returned. Juliet took notice of the beach's guidelines as to no one can be on the grounds after a certain hour. So while no one was around she entered with caution and made her way far down to a cozy secluded area. She took out a couple of bed sheets—which she'd stolen from the Motel-8—laid them over the sand and settled in under the stars. The billions of stars about the dark sky were so wondrous that they almost made her forget that she only had eight dollars to her name. But still, she held no regrets in leaving Boise.

Juliet cuddled up for warmth dressed head to toe in her heaviest clothes; the night's temperature had dropped below 60 degrees. I have to make some cash, she thought. I have to find a job. Minutes later, as the ocean waves crashed upon the rocks and shore, Juliet drifted off to sleep. Tomorrow was another day.

*　*　　*

Long Beach proved to live up to its name, although Romero never actually made it out to the sands but he watched as cars and Jeeps hauled surfboards and jet skis up and down the avenues as he would walk from McDonalds. Every morning he would try to catch breakfast but he'd always miss it by minutes, so he would settle for his two chicken sandwiches, small fries, and Hi-C orange drink. Most of Romero's time went to writing his novel. He would brainstorm for hours just mumbling to himself as he paced back and forth, then it would hit him and he'd type away as if in a zone. Romero's book was about a young man on the mean streets of Chicago trying to overcome life's obstacles. It was an urban novel that he wanted to self-publish and shop around to some of the big California publishing houses. All Romero wanted was that one chance. If his work was as good as some said, and he put it into the hands of someone great… The sky was the limit.

Later on that night after many hours of word play and clever chapter climaxes, Romero was once again hungry and decided to head down the block to McDonalds. The city was alive with night life and the cool breeze felt good compared to his motel's atmosphere. As he walked the sidewalks which were dirty and grimy he was approached by streetwalkers and drug hustlers. Hookers catcalled to him all the time and some nights it was hard for him to turn them down, but Romero couldn't lose focus because one night of "tricking-off" could lead to not only him spending his only cash but possibly getting jacked, killed, or set up.

Once he had purchased his food he headed back. He was hungry so he walked with haste taking an alternate route through a short alleyway. The alley smelled of piss and trash as steam billowed out of manholes. Rats scurried about as cats gave chase for their late-night snacks.

Then, just as he could see his street ahead, he was startled by a scream. Romero looked down the left-side alleyway and could see a short, skinny white man. He was standing over a small white female on the ground. The man then punched the female in the head making her fall back on the dirty ground. The woman cried out in pain as the man gave her a hard kick to her midsection which made her fold over clutching her stomach in agony.

"Stinking bitch!" the man spat. "Whores don't tease."

Damn, Romero thought as he shook his head, proceeding about his business.

"Help me! Please, he's gonna rape me!" the woman shouted. Romero paused. The white man turned and saw him.

"Just mind your own business pal, keep it moving," he told Romero. The small woman tried to scurry away but received a shoving kick to her butt that sent her crashing into some trash cans. Fuck! Romero thought. He hated to get involved but where he was from, a nigga didn't take too kindly to rape... on any level. So, with his food in hand, he ran down the left-side alleyway and without warning, he shoulder-rushed the unsuspecting man in the back. The force from the blow knocked the wind out of the man and sent him flying forward where he crashed head first into a sloppy stack of trash bags. The man was laid out cold, but he wasn't dead but unconscious. Romero was breathing heavy with adrenaline, the small female was in a corner next to a dumpster looking over at him with wide eyes. Romero looked down at her.

"You aight?" he asked her. The small female pushed her hair out of her face and wiped away tears. When the girl nodded yes he nodded as well and simply continued on his way. She followed.

Chapter 2

Juliet was so thankful for her rescuer; there was no telling what that creep would have done if the guy wouldn't have shown up. She felt so stupid, why was she down in the dirt with a creepo like that anyway? Oh, because she had no money, no food or place to sleep. Juliet didn't know why she felt she could make some fast cash becoming a wannabe hooker, giving handjobs only wouldn't hold over a pussy-hungry man. That's what was wrong with the guy in the alley, he wanted more than hand service and so he decided to take what he wanted. But now he was out cold, dead even, and it was all because some guy had compassion enough to step in. She wanted to thank this hero.

"Hey!" Juliet called. She galloped out the alley behind the man and did her best to keep up. "Hey you, thank you for doing that," she said, coming up on his side shouldering her book bag.

"It's all good," Romero said. "Just be careful next time."

"Well… Well, here's the thing. I'm not a real hooker, see—"

"What are you? Part-timing?" he cut in.

"Well, something like that. He promised to give me twenty bucks for a handjob but got frisky, ya know."

"Well you good now. I'll holla atcha," Romero said kinda brushing her off. He didn't want some dirty little streetwalker tryna run a con game on him. Hell, he helped and now he wanted to get back to his own world. But Juliet persisted, she also smelled his food and couldn't help but to want whatever it was he had in his bag.

"You like McDonalds, huh?" she asked walking next to him. Romero frowned with puzzlement. "I love Big Macs, is that what you got?" she asked.

"No, chicken sandwiches," he told her, switching the bag into his other hand.

"Oh, I like those too, and their pies. Those two-for-a-dollar apple pies."

"I got those too. Look shorty," he stopped with irritation. "What do you want?"

Juliet was saddened that she made the guy upset. She felt like a lowlife. They stood in awkward silence for a moment on the dark sidewalk, two strangers in the night. "I was just wondering is all," she began. "Thank you for what you did back there." Juliet turned and started walking away. Romero felt bad as he watched and shook his head in dismay. The white girl looked lost and harmless. Back in the city of Chicago the guys would consider running into a little white chick a potential "come-up," but he wasn't as cold-hearted as his guys and held no ill intent for the female. As Juliet walked down the street with no destination in mind, she heard the man call to her.

"'Ay, shorty!'"

She instantly turned to find him holding out the bag of food.

"You hungry?" he asked.

"Yeah… I can eat," she responded.

"Aight, come wit' me, cause I'm gonna watch you eat this shit," he told her. Juliet smiled and galloped back over to him. Romero was looking at her like: Why is she so damn chipper? She just almost got raped.

"You can watch me; I'll eat it, I promise. Where are we going?" she asked.

"To my spot. What's yo' name, shorty?"

"Juliet," she told him. "What's yours?"

"Romero, but everybody back home call me Rome."

"Wow… Romero and Juliet, just like in the fairy tales," she said with dreamy eyes. Romero frowned.

"Whatever, come on."

They didn't speak much all the way back to the motel room. The young girl followed behind him in silence and entered into his room as he held open the door for her. Romero's room was kind of messy. Old fast food bags and cups were all over and his bed was unmade. He locked the door and led the way over to the card table where his laptop was. He picked up a small trashcan and pushed all the trash in, clearing the tabletop. Juliet stood by him with her bag on her shoulder. She glanced around the small room and was okay with being there alone with a stranger. She didn't know why but she trusted that the young guy was good.

"Go ahead and sit down," he told her as he began to remove the food from the bag. Juliet did and sat her book bag on the carpet next to her. He placed a chicken sandwich and a pie in front of her just before he did the same for himself while also taking a seat.

14

"Thank you," she told him. Juliet wasted no time and began eating like she was a savage. She hadn't eaten in over fifty-two hours and she was starved. Romero just watched in amazement as she devoured half her sandwich in seconds. He didn't even get to tell her what he had the people putt on it just in case she didn't eat specific things, but she didn't seem to care, she just ate. So Romero just sat back and observed her. She was cute, he thought. Dirty, but cute. Juliet was 5'4", 121 pounds, dirty-blonde hair, and milky clear complexion, with blazing green eyes. She reminded Romero of Topanga from the 90s kids' show "Boy Meets World." Only thing was this female wasn't large-chested nor were her lips as full. The best physical feature which he only got a quick look at was her butt. It looked plump. It was time for Romero to pry.

"Why you out on the streets, shorty?" he asked boldly. Juliet chewed her food, she was so damn hungry but the food she munched was hitting the spot. She spoke with a mouthful.

"I'm a rolling stone," she told him.

"What? Rolling stone? The hell does that mean? What, you ain't from Cali?"

"Uh-uh… Idaho. I left home to get away from my old life. I figured California was the best place to start fresh. Thing is… I didn't have a solid plan so I ran out of money pretty quick," she explained.

"So you started hooking for handjobs for extra money?"

"Mhmm, I'm not proud and I'm no pro, but hey… a girl's got to eat." She went back to eating and polished off her chicken. Next she slid out the pie and bit it.

"How old are you, shorty?" he asked.

"Seventeen now. How old are you?"

"Twenty-one. So you came to Cali all alone?"

"Yup, just me, myself, and I," she told him, chewing.

"How long you been out here?"

"Umm… about three weeks."

"When you run out of money?"

"About three or four days in," she told him.

"Damn, where you been living since then?"

"The beach, mainly. My other bag is stashed down the shore."

Romero shook his head, her story so far was sad. He pushed over his pie to her and she smiled before eating it as well.

"So Romero, are you from Long Beach?" she asked.

"Chicago."

"Oh really? Chitown. I always wanted to visit there. What are you doing way out West?"

"I'm writing a novel. I thought coming out here would give me some inspiration," he told her.

"A book? Wow, you're a writer? That's cool. How long have you been out here?"

"Not too long, a week or so." Romero watched as she finished off the second apple pie. She then pointed to an old fountain drink sitting next to his computer. He shrugged. Juliet took the top off the drink and drank the Pepsi. It was warm and watered down but she didn't care.

"So, what are you gonna do when tomorrow comes? And the days after that? Pull another trick?" he asked.

Juliet shrugged. She didn't really know. All she knew was she wasn't going back to her dad's. "Maybe," she began. "Handjobs aren't that bad. I'm doing my best but no one will hire me out here."

Romero felt bad for her. She seemed like a sweet chick, kind of goofy but sweet. He couldn't just turn her away, back out into the streets. The thought of her taking chances with "thirsty" men in alleyways for pennies was crazy. She was lucky she wasn't on the mean streets of Chicago because by now she'd be strung out on drugs going all the way in the backseats of many cars, and her pimp would get every red cent. So he did what he felt was right.

"Look, I don't usually do this but… you can crash here if you want to."

"Really?" she said, surprised.

"Fo'sho, but let me be clear. I don't play no games, it's just you, feel me? No other mufuckas come to my spot."

"All right, cause there ain't no one else. Anymore rules?"

"Yeah. No drugs," he said.

"I don't do drugs. I mean, I have smoked weed but not since I got out here."

"Good. I smoke weed, just not right now. Anyways, you see I only got one bed, I ain't sleepin' on the floor, shorty, so… you got to do what you do."

"That's fine, shit, I've been sleeping on sand for almost a month. Anything else?"

Romero thought for a moment. "Yeah, this is my spot so you can only come and go when I'm here. I ain't givin' you my key, so if you leave and come back and I gone… then it's a waiting game for you."

"Fine, what else?" she said, smiling.

"Uh… yeah, look, when I write I'm gon' need you to not bother me. I be in my zone and I don't need you to mess me up," he told her bluntly.

"Fine, no talking while you work. Anything else?"

Romero was kinda perplexed by the girl, it was as if she was cool with everything he said. He wondered was she like all the rest of those white chicks who liked niggas and would do what their man said. He always wanted a white girl like that, but he was just thinking that's how the male mind worked. "That's it for now but if something come up I'll let you know," he told her. Romero then grabbed his sandwich, opened it, and took a bite. He picked up the remote and turned on the TV. "Family Guy" was on. Romero handed her the remote before he picked up his laptop and moved over to the bed where he plopped down and continued to eat. They both sat in silence as she channel surfed. Finally she landed back on "Family Guy" and they sat and watched the episode. Romero and Juliet giggled and occasionally made comments about the show. Twenty minutes later after the show was ending and another was coming on, Juliet turned and asked, "May I take a shower?"

"Yeah, go ahead, there's towels and all that in there," he told her, gesturing to the bathroom. Juliet gathered her bag, handed him the remote, and entered the bathroom, shutting the door behind her. Moments later the shower could be heard. Romero took his computer and did a little bit of chapter work, for some reason he was inspired.

In the bathroom Juliet disrobed and got in the shower. The hot water felt so good on her filthy flesh. She was glad that she had the luck of meeting Romero. He was a nice guy, and handsome too. He was tall, dark, and kind. Crazy thing was she hadn't had any black friends her whole life, hell, she hardly knew any black folks. Sure, they were in Idaho but she never really had any interactions with them. But she liked Romero. She liked him a lot. She wondered if he had a girlfriend back in Chicago. She could see herself dating a black guy. She smiled to herself as she soaped her body and washed days' worth of grime off her skin. Romero and Juliet, she thought. It had a nice ring to it.

* * *

As the rising sun shined into the motel room, its rays hit Romero's face and made him squint. Seconds later he began to wake and stretch with a wide yawn. When he opened his eyes, he took a few moments to gather his thoughts. Then he remembered her. Romero fell asleep last night while Juliet was in the shower. He popped up and looked on the floor but she wasn't there. Then he got up and went for the bathroom and found she wasn't there either. He came back into the main room and saw her book bag still there. Maybe she went to get her other bag, he thought.

Romero stood in the bathroom taking a leak when a knock at the door came. He finished up and answered it. When he opened the door a fully dressed, fresh-faced Juliet was there. She smiled brightly and in her hand she held two bowls of dry cereal, two cups of milk, and two glazed donuts.

"I'm sorry if I woke you, but I was up this morning and decided to take a walk down to the beach to get my other bag. When I came back I noticed this place offered free continental breakfast, so I hooked us up. It was the least I could do for you being so nice to me and all."

Juliet made her way past him and headed for the table. Romero was still kind of sleepy as he closed the door, watching her walk through. She was dressed in a pair of "Daisy Duke" shorts and a halter top. Her long hair was pulled back into a ponytail and she wore a halfway decent pair of shoes. Romero went back into the bathroom and started washing his face and brushing his teeth. He didn't even know the motel had free breakfast. If he would have known that he could have saved himself some money. When he was done, he came out and found the table set with a bowl of cereal and a donut on either side. Juliet sat waiting as if for him. He sat down.

"Damn, I appreciate this," he said, starting to eat. He nodded with delighted approval as he munched on the soft, sweet donut. Juliet was happy to see him happy and then she began to eat.

"So what's on the agenda today?" she asked him.

"Same old thing, find my writing hole and fall in."

"You mean typing hole," she corrected harmlessly.

"Whatever, as long as it gets me to the next chapter. What's your plans?" he asked, chewing.

"Well, I was gonna go job hunting again, but after that I was hoping you would come to the beach with me," she said to him.

"Beach? I don't know about that one. Water ain't really my thing. I'm not really into water games."

"You don't have to swim or play games, you could just come to be out. You can watch me splash around. Come on, you can take a little break, can't you?"

"I don't know," he said, leaning back with his bowl.

"Please, just for a little while," she begged.

"Ain't you tired of the beach?" he asked.

"No, I love it, it's alive and fun. Come on, Romero. I want someone I know to be there with me. We can lay in the sand and get to know each other better. You can tell me your story and I can tell you mine."

Romero rolled his eyes. He didn't want to go but maybe he would be inspired by something he saw. He gave in. "Aight, I'll go, but I can't be out too long cause I'm on a deadline."

Juliet was overjoyed and clapped as she stood. "Thank you. I'll be back in about two hours," she said as she left out of the motel room. When she was gone Romero noticed something else. The room was clean. She had cleaned up all the trash and placed all his tossed clothes neatly in a pile in the corner. Damn, he thought as he finished his cereal. She just might be a keeper.

*   *   *

Juliet filled out several applications around the area. She felt more joy than she did a few days ago when she found five dollars in the sand. She felt good when she saw how appreciative Romero was when she gave him his breakfast. Then getting him to agree to join her down at the beach was even better. She was taken by him for some reason. Even though there was much more that remained to be known about him, she didn't mind. She would find out who he was once they conversed later on.   After filling out over five applications, Juliet headed back to the motel. She figured it had to be well after one o'clock. When she knocked on the door, she was let in and Romero instantly went back to the table where his computer was. She didn't say a word, just came in and took a seat on the edge of his bed. They sat in silence for a while with the TV off and the sound of him tapping away at the keyboard. Ten minutes later he closed down his computer and addressed her.

"How was job hunting?" he asked with crossed legs.

"Application aplenty were filled out, that's all I can say. I gave them this room number, I hope you don't mind."

"That coo' wit' me. Anyways, you ready to roll out?" he asked. Romero looked at her bare stomach and the rest of her body. Her nipples could be seen protruding through her top. She had some little B-cups.

"Yeah, I'm ready if you are," she told him. Juliet noticed him scanning her body. He could probably see her nipples harden because of the coolness of the air conditioner. She didn't mind though. She hoped he liked what he saw.

"How far's the beach, cause I don't have no car," he asked.

"Not four blocks away, down on Rosen Avenue."

"Right, well, get yo' stuff together, bathing suit or whatever," he told her, slipping on his shoes. Juliet got up and retrieved a simple blue bikini top from her bag. She quickly went into the bathroom and came back out with it on. She grabbed her large beach towel and folded it over her forearm.

"All set." She smiled. They headed out for the beach. It would change both of their lives forever.

Chapter 3

The beach was packed. There had to be a thousand people. Everyone smiling, playing, tanning, eating, and sightseeing. Romero had been to the beach back in Chicago but it was nothing compared to what he was experiencing now. Besides all the people on the sand there were more outside on the boardwalk. Those folks walked with loved ones or roller-skated, skateboarded, bought food at vendor carts, or shopped at the strip stores. Romero and Juliet found a nice spot and bedded down. He felt overdressed in his black jean shorts, socks, Nike shoes, and short-sleeve dress shirt, so he removed everything but his shorts and tank top. Romero was no bodybuilder, but he was fit. He was 6'2", 182 pounds and prided himself on having a "Trey Songz" physique. Although he looked nothing like the R &B star, he was good looking enough for the block chicks back home to call him "Terrence Jerkins" because he sort of favored the retired 106 & Park host, only difference was he was darker and had no money. Romero sat down on the large towel Juliet had brought and watched as she stepped out of her shorts and was in her two-piece. She had a bad little body, and his mind couldn't help but wonder how soft her ass might feel. But he was faced with a bit of a moral dilemma because she not only was underage but was also a runaway. He wondered if he could get in trouble if the girl's people sent out missing person flyers and all that junk and finally found her cross-country staying with a black man from Chicago in a motel. Even though seventeen was close to being legal and twenty-one was still young… the law was real picky about situations like that. I better be careful, he thought.

"Man, it's blazin' out here, girl," he complained as the sun's hot temperature beat down on him. Juliet sighed with her hands on her hips and smiled at him.

"Well then… you better come splash in the cool water," she told him. She instantly took off running towards the ocean with jack-rabbit speed. Romero watched as she made it to the water and dived in head first, seconds later she emerged about ten feet in. Juliet pushed her wet hair back, wiped water from her face and waved to Romero. He respectfully returned the wave with a half smile that read: Hey… whatever.

After about five minutes of baking in the sun, Romero didn't think the water was so bad, but still he dismissed the thought because he had no trunks. Moments later, Juliet jogged back up the shore. She looked like one of those white kids from the TV commercials advertising beach wear.

"Did you see me out there? I waved to you," she said. She removed a motel tower from her bag and began to dry herself. The cool water mixed with the air made her nipples protrude once again and Romero tried not to stare.

"Yeah, I saw you, and I waved back," he told her. "Man, I'm hungry like a mufucka, I'm finna go out to the boardwalk to that hotdog stand. You wanna come or..."

"I'll come," Juliet answered quick as she dried her hair. "Will you buy me a hotdog too?"

"Come on now, yeah 'mma buy you one. Look... you wit' me now, you ain't got nothing so I got you. We gon' eat together for as long as you stay with me at the room."

Juliet smiled, nodding. She then wrapped the towel around her waist and helped pull Romero up on his feet. At the hotdog stand he bought them both a foot-long with the works and sodas. They walked the boardwalk eating and chatting about life. Juliet told him in deep detail about her home situation with her father. She held nothing back and was unashamed in telling him. Romero was no stranger to sad stories but for some reason hers seemed sadder because she was now in his life for a time. Romero in return revealed his life and upbringing. Juliet was fascinated by his story and couldn't relate to all the wild things he had seen or been through, but they did have many things in common. Both of them were April babies. They both loved movies of all kinds. They hated seafood but liked fish. Both wanted to be rich and have a family. Romero and Juliet had found common ground and were building a friendship. They were enjoying one another's company. As they strolled, they came upon a small trinket stand that sold all sorts of things; hats, sunglasses, mood rings, bracelets, necklaces, and other wacky things. Romero picked up a small digital camera and looked it over. Seconds later the stand owner approached him.

"Mighty fine camera there," the short, fat man said, grinning. He was dressed in Tydy from head to toe. He looked like an old hippie. "Tell ya what… you buy the camera and I'll toss in a free computer upload cord, how's that sound?" The hippie's sales pitch was weak but Romero needed a camera that could upload potential book cover images for his project. Just then, Juliet came to his side. She leaned on his shoulder like they were a couple.

"How much you asking for?" Romero asked.

"For you? …Forty dollars," the man told him.

"Forty you say?" Romero said, examining the camera again. "It's a deal if you toss in one of them teddy bears for her."

Juliet was shocked and happy to be thought of. She had her eyes on the large white bear with the pink heart on its chest. The hippie salesman thought for a moment, then he extended his hand to Romero. "Bud, you got a deal. Little lady, choose your bear."

Juliet stepped up and pointed to the one she wanted and received it. Romero pulled out two bills and paid the man.

"Thank you," Juliet said to him as they made it back to their spot on the sand.

"It's all good."

"Did you change your mind about swimming?" she asked as she set her bear down and took off her towel.

"Hell nah."

"Come on, Romey. Can you at least come down and get your feet wet? You can take some pictures of me doing handstands and stuff," she begged.

"I don't care about doing that, I'm just not swimming."

Juliet was glad to get him to do that, so she took him by the hand and led him down the shore. When they were at the water's edge, Juliet ran into the shallow waters and posed. Romero clicked away and she switched poses like an amateur model. She did handstands in the water, cartwheels out of the water. Dived with the waving hands, and acted silly. Taking a seat at the water's edge, he scanned through all the pictures he took and smiled at them. He shook his head at the goofy face she had made when a wave crashed onto her back.

"Did you get some good ones?" Juliet asked as she came trotting out of the ocean. She stood in front of him and wrung out her hair.

"I got a few crazy ones," he told her. Juliet took a seat next to him and looked at the pictures of herself on the digital screen. She blushed as she saw how goofy she looked in some of them.

"So Romero Hinton... you got a girlfriend in Chicago?" she asked, handing the camera back.

"Nope, no female. Ain't none worthy. They all be on bullshit where I live, they all disloyal," he told her. "But what about you? You got a dude back home?" he asked. Juliet shook her head.

"No, never had a boyfriend before."

"Get the hell out of here," Romero said in disbelief.

"Honest to God," she told him. "I'm a social freak back home. My best friend was my cat who got ran over last year. I had guys who seemed to like me but nothing ever became of them, plus my dad would have killed me."

"Wow... that's crazy," he said. Silence fell between them and they simply watched the ocean. It was almost four o'clock and the day was slowly coming to its close. Romero had to get back to work.

"Well, stick wit' ya boy for the next few weeks and you gon' be aight. A job gon' pop and you gon' be on yo' way," he assured her.

"And you'll publish your book and sell the rights to a major studio and make millions," she assured him right back.

"Damn right," he smiled proudly. "Aight, let's bounce. I got to get back to it." They gathered their things and headed back to the motel.

* * *

"Fuck, man!" Romero shouted in anger as he paced the motel floor. "I knew I shouldn't have fuckin' went to no beach!" Juliet sat on the edge of the bed with her head down like a sad child. She was broken-hearted that Romero lost his billfold. About halfway back to the room, Romero noticed that his entire wallet was gone. He was so frantic that he just took off running without word back to the beach. Juliet called after him but she could only run after him. When she finally made it there she found Romero standing with his wallet in hand. He was looking out into the ocean. The wallet was intact but someone had taken all his money, and from what Juliet knew it was well over a thousand dollars. She felt bad. She felt responsible because true enough if she wouldn't have begged him to go then the money would never have gotten stolen.

"Fuck, man! I don't got shit, not a dollar! The fuck am I gonna do now? Now what? How can I feed myself? I can't even get back to the city now." Romero was so angry that he was tired, so he sat down at the head of his bed. He placed his face in his hands and wanted to cry. The room fell silent for a while, the air wasn't even on. Romero didn't know what to do, he couldn't call home for money because his mother counted on him for help, she didn't have hundreds to send him over the wire. The day was now night. The sun was only a glow on the ocean's surface as the city's streetlights illuminated the darkness. Romero's head was banging like a war drum, so he slipped his shoes off and curled up on the bed. Juliet sat there on the bed's edge for a while unmoved, then she got up and went and took a shower. When she was done she came back out dressed in another pair of bikini bottoms and a large t-shirt that hung to her knees. As she made up her pallet on the floor she looked to Romero and saw that he was still awake. Minutes later she was on her pallet curled up at the foot of the bed.

"Rome," she called softly. He didn't answer. "Rome," she called softly once more.

"Man... what up?" he said low with irritation.

"I'm sorry you lost your money. I know it's my fault. Please don't kick me out," she said. A moment of silence fell.

"Man... Juliet, I'm messed up in the head right now. I ain't gon' kick you out, man... it's just... shit's real right now," he told her. Silence fell once more. Juliet was glad to hear that she could stay. She wanted to help him somehow but she didn't have anything to give. She could only think of one thing.

"Rome," she called lightly.

"What up?"

"Can I come lay with you for tonight?" she asked.

"I don't give no fuck... come on," he told her without care. Juliet got up and he scooted over allowing her to have laying room, but as he did she simply came over to him and snuggled up on him. Juliet lay on her side with her head on the right side of Romero's chest. She felt comfortable there with him, safe even.

"What's gonna happen now?" she asked him low.

"I don't even know... try to finish the book and submit it to Google's CreateSpace, see if it sells."

"But what about in the meantime?"

"I don't know. I need to find some type of hustle game. I'll come up with something… I don't got no choice," he told her. He placed his arm around her and rubbed her shoulder. She smelled fresh like soap and baby lotion. Juliet cuddled closer, placing her right hand on his stomach. She smelled his deodorant and musky-sweet aroma. She began to rub his abdomen. Romero could feel his hormones rising. He could tell that something sexual could jump off at any moment. He wanted to relieve some stress, he had to or he'd go crazy and strong-arm rob somebody on the streets. Fuck the age gap and the law, he thought, he was going in.

"You might as well go on head and grab dick," he boldly told her. Juliet stopped rubbing. She heard perfectly well what he said but human nature made her ask anyway.

"Hmm?" she said with a nervous tone. He repeated.

"Go on head and grab dick since you rubbin' already."

Juliet did what he told her and slid her hand into his shorts and gripped his thick, warm hard-on. "Like this?" she asked. Her touch sent shockwaves through his body. It was about to go down.

"Hell yeah like that. Pull that mufucka out and get down," he said to her.

"Huh?" she asked, not knowing his street lingo.

"Pull dick out and suck dat bitch," he told her more plainly. So Juliet pulled her hand out, undid his shorts, zipped them down and up sprang his long, brown cock. She was nervous as hell. She had never "given head" to anyone by choice. Yes, she had sucked her dirtbag father off a time or two but it was forced… this was different, this was willing sex with someone she liked. Juliet leaned over his lap and took his eight-inch dick into her small white hand, then she opened her mouth and engulfed him like a Popsicle. Romero bit his bottom lip as the wet warmth of her mouth covered his member all the way down to the base. Juliet began to go slow on him, deep-throating his dick each time. Down… up… down… up she went.

"Shit, girl," he said with pleasure. "Scoot that ass back here some." Juliet did. She positioned herself so that her butt was facing upward. Then she could feel him rubbing her butt and squeezing. Then he pulled and pulled until her large shirt was up and bunched up on the small of her back, her ass was now exposed. Romero reached between her milky white legs and palmed

26

her pussy. He rubbed her warm vaginal mound through the fabric of her blue bikini bottoms.

"Mmm," Juliet moaned softly as he did. "Mmm."

Romero pulled the bottoms to the side and slipped his middle finger deep into her wet pussy hole. Juliet's eyes widened and she—just for a moment—took him out of her mouth to say, "Oh… it's in me now."

Romero began to finger-drill her as she blew him good. Then, when it seemed she couldn't concentrate on sucking anymore, he stopped her. Romero was hot now, ready for entry.

"Get naked," he told her. He stood up on the side of the bed and took off all of his clothes. Juliet did the same and was fully naked on the bed. Romero stood and admired her smooth little body. Her titties were small and perky with Milk Dud–sized areolas. Her pubic area was nicely groomed as if she had just shaved it that night.

"Come here," he told her. She came to him on her knees and by her face he brought her up to meet his lips. They kissed wet and deep, Romero didn't care if he was tasting his own juices, he wanted to kiss. When they stopped, he held her there, looking into her eyes.

"You okay with all this?" he asked her. Juliet was. In fact, she had never been so sure.

"I'm okay with whatever you want," she told him with a sexy smile. "Just don't hurt me."

Romero frowned. "Shorty… you all good. Turn over; let me get it from the back," he told her.

Juliet turned and positioned herself on her knees. Romero knelt on the bed behind her and gave her a pillow to hug onto. He rubbed his hand from her lower spine all the way to her shoulder as he readied for entry. Then, with cock in hand, he pushed the plump bell of his dickhead into the front gates of her pussy. She was tight. Romero gripped her hips and drove himself in a little deeper. Juliet cried out with pleasure and pain as his large rod went in only halfway. Romero didn't want to hurt her so he put both hands on his hips and allowed her to take control.

"Go ahead and push back on it, lil' mama," he told her.

Juliet did as she was told and slowly pushed herself back onto him until she could feel his dick fully inside her pussy's limited space. Juliet's mouth hung open with closed eyes as she began to fuck herself without help.

Romero watched as her white ass went slowly back and forth, making most of his dick disappear inside her. He could see and feel her becoming more loose and wet. He wanted control again.

"You good, shorty?" he asked.

"Mhmm, yeah," she said, sounding completely stimulated.

"You ready for me to beat dat pussy up?"

"Yeah," she said, pulling her hair out of her face. She then looked back as best she could as Romero took her by the hips. He pulled her back and pushed himself forward. She watched. He then just began a nice pace, pumping in and out of her. Juliet's mouth hung open wide as she looked back at him with a shaking body. Then she cried out loudly with delight and buried her face in the pillow. Clap-slap-clap went the repeating sound of flesh on flesh. Romero sped up and was pounding her good from behind.

"Oooh," she moaned. "Oooh yesss, yesss."

"Uh huh, uh huh, what's my name, what's my name?"

"Romey, Romey, Romey, oooh, it's good baby, yeah."

"You wanna be my bitch, huh? You wanna be wit' Rome?" he asked aggressively as he pounded her pussy.

"Yeah—oooh yeah, I wanna be—I wanna be your bitch, mmm—yeah, I wanna be your bitch, Romey." Juliet was in the ninth level of bliss. She said whatever he wanted to hear. All she knew was that his cock was hitting a spot within her that drove her wild and she didn't want him to ever stop.

"Shit! Lil' mama, I'm finna nut, you gon' let me nut on them titties? You gon' let me bust on them titties?" he asked as his ball began to surge. Juliet didn't say a thing. She just got off and faced him. She pressed her small breasts together for him as he jerked himself off. Juliet looked up into his eyes as he reached his tipping point and shot lines of warm cum all on her chest and neck. Out of breath and exhausted, Romero came boldly down and kissed her deep while her chest remained spattered with semen. Then he went to the washroom, wet a towel and returned so they could clean off. When they were done, Romero clicked on the AC and they lay in the bed together under the covers.

"You were so good," she told him. Juliet was smiling from ear to ear as she held onto him like a child.

"Mhmm. You were taking that D like a champ, too."

"I know, right? You were hitting that spot inside me," she told him. Romero was proud of his sex-game, he was flattered that she loved what he put on her. He didn't mind having his ego stroked.

"Romey," she called softly. "When we were doing it you asked if I wanted to be your bitch… I know I said yes but what did you mean by it?"

"First off, I don't mean bitch as being disrespectful. You see, in my hood, when a guy say, 'I'm with my bitch tonight.' He's saying, 'I'm with my girlfriend, my number one baby.' So when I said what I said, I was saying do you wanna be my girl? My number one baby? My bitch?"

"So are you really asking me to be your girlfriend?" she asked for clarification.

"That depends on you, lil' mama. Are you willing to be 100% loyal to your man?"

"To you—yeah," she said.

"Well, then it's me and your world. Say that," he told her.

Juliet didn't quite understand until he told her again. "Oh… it's you and my world," she repeated with honor.

"There you go… now all we have to do is find a hustle to make some 'ends.' You wit' me, Juliet?"

"Yes Romey, I'm with you," she assured him.

"Aight… let's get some sleep. Tomorrow we hustle."

Chapter 4

Juliet could only sleep halfway through the night. She had bad dreams which she had from time to time, dreams of her father dressed as the devil. He would come into her room with hellfire behind him and demonic eyes. He would have a snake penis that tried to bite her.

By the light of the television, Juliet lay against Romero's warm body as he slept. She didn't know for sure but she felt she was "in love" with him. She wanted to be with him. She had a strong, deep connection to serve him. She felt she could and would do anything for him. Why? She didn't know. Juliet wanted to do something to help them both with their many dilemmas. She had a solution for the short-time, but she didn't know how Romero would take it. Like he basically said to her, they were now a team. But Romero was black, and from the mean streets of Chicago, and his tales were not farfetched from her plan. He liked her, she knew. He liked being inside her, she also knew. So she would bring her plan to him. She just had to phrase her words with care.

"Rome," she called lightly to him with a shake. "Rome."

"Hmm—huh, what?" he said sleepily.

"Um... I've been thinking. I can get you your money."

"Oh yeah?" he said, clearing his throat. "How you gon' do that? Jerk a thousand guys off?" Romero said it only being sarcastic, but the answer he got blew his mind. After a brief pause, she answered.

"If that's what you tell me," she said.

"Say what?"

"I'd do it for us if you asked. I'd go all the way if I knew it would help us."

Romero was puzzled in the darkness and sat up and clicked on the nightstand light. Juliet sat up as well and looked him in the eyes.

"Hold on... whatchu sayin'? Cause it sound like you sayin' you'd sell some pussy," he said to her with confusion.

Juliet didn't answer. She just held a heartening look on her face. Romero rubbed his head, blown away. She was saying what he thought.

"Shit, Juliet… I mean… damn, you would get out there like that for me?" he asked. She shrugged.

"For us, I would," she told him. "If you protected me."

Romero shook his head a bit. He always wondered about "pimping" a female. He had homies back home who had cousins and uncles who did it for a living. He never understood how a female could sell her body 24/7, through rain, sleet, and snow, and just hand over all the money she earned fucking and sucking strangers to give it all to some pimp. But now, he himself was faced with the wild opportunity to guide and use a willing female's body like an endless money tree. Romero had to go about this the right way, the smart and safe way.

"Are you mad that I—"

"No," he cut her off. "I'm not mad… I'm just getting my thoughts together. So you'll really do this?"

"I really would, if you promised to be around just in case a situation pops up."

"And you talkin' 'bout all the way?"

"If the money's right," she told him.

Romero sighed, looking at the dark clock. It was after one a.m.

"Aight… aight look, I'm wit' it, but… if we gon' do this, then we got to be smart. We got to be safe and you got to push pride to the side and do exactly as I tell you. You feel me?"

"Yeah," she said, becoming enthralled because he was in. Romero got out of the bed and stood before her in just his boxers. He was about to give her the game as he felt he knew it. Juliet sat back and listened.

"Aight, look… as a female you have to know one thing and that's men love pussy, and in most cases they prefer young chicks. Juliet, you got to know that you are young, good looking and have power over a shitload of thirsty-ass studs. They wanna fuck you, plain and simple, but… you can make they ass pay to play. Look, I ain't yo' pimp or shit like that… I'm yo' nigga, and as yo' nigga, I wanna see you make the most bread for the service you give out. Just because you fuckin' other dudes for money don't mean you ain't mines because you are. If I don't like a stud then I shut it down. Feel me?"

"Mhmm," she said, listening close. He continued.

"Now… peep game. I ain't gonna have you out on the corners like some dirty, cheap hoe who risking getting locked up by the 'sting-boys.' We

31

gon' use the computer and the social networks to pull in clientele."

"You mean like Facebook and stuff?" she interjected.

"Right," he told her. "Like Facebook and other chat lines."

"That sounds safer," she added.

"I know. Peep game. We gon' deal with this area only, Cali. Have you ever seen 'To Catch a Predator'?" he asked.

"Uh huh."

"Them mufuckas be thirsty for pussy, and they be making trips. Imagine if each one of them mufuckas came to pay… and there was no sting operation… man, old girl would be filthy right with bread. We got to have them lined up like that… if you feel you can handle it." He paused to see if she had a comment.

"I don't know, Romey, I mean I'm no pro, I know what to do and how to do it but I don't know how much I can handle. I don't want to do it with some fat nasty old dude. I at least want whoever to be clean looking," she told him.

"Right, and you gon' have yo' application process when a stud come on to you. If he coo' den you good. If he bogus then you pass, simple as that."

"All right. So what about prices and stuff?" she asked.

"Good question, uhh… It's really about how you feel. You see you got to master the art of reading how thirsty a stud is. If he traveled from long distance then he may pay more, especially if he feel you underage. But if he local he may want to pay less because he feel he can get a ten-dollar hoe off the strip. It's up to you ultimately, but if you want a rate from me… I say fifty for head and a hundred for sex, one-fifty for the full package. What you think?"

"Sounds all right. What about anal? I don't think I'd like that," she told him.

"Then we stick to head and sex, or a ten-dollar handjob. I'm gonna work the kinks out more later, but right now I got to school you about your power."

Over the next three hours, Romero gave Juliet the game. He told her the ins and outs, the ups and downs, and every other way he could think of. He ran elaborate scenarios with her dealing with police, unruly tricks, and how to haggle. He even gave her tips on how to cheat at giving a man head, a trick which was done on him plenty of times back in Chicago. It was ten sucks and five jerk-offs. The method saved a female from sucking so much and allowed her to dirty talk the client into climax. Juliet soaked up all the information he gave to her. She took mental notes and made sure she stored key points.

Then came the website part. Romero placed her on Facebook and Craigslist. Both of her introductions basically said the same things, except on Craigslist the sexual proposition was less subtle. On Juliet's Facebook page, Romero posted all the photos he took of her at the beach, even a few more wholesome ones in the motel room. And on her message board, she dropped hints, words that pulled in "creeps" from around the area. Words like "wild" and "open," "young" and "willing." And lines like "I love to be wined and dined," "looking to find a man who can handle my wild side."

Then, over on Craigslist, Romero posted a provocative picture of Juliet posed in her bikini on the bed. Her ad message said lines such as "looking to have a good time with real men" and "we can do the nasty as long as I'm wined and dined first."

Romero also cruised Facebook and looked for as many single guys in the area of Long Beach, and when he read their profiles he determined if they were potential "creeps" or not. Once he did that he friend requested them.

Around five o'clock is when he and Juliet decided to call it quits. They both jumped in the shower together and as they washed one another, they ended up having sex again. When they were done, they got back into bed and fell back to sleep.

*   *   *

Once again Juliet was the first to rise out of bed. When she awoke the clock read 11:10. The AC had the room chilly so she turned it on "Fan" as she pulled on her panties and the rest of her clothes. Grabbing the room key, she went down to the front lobby and stocked up on free breakfast. The Asian desk clerk gave her the stinky-eye as Juliet took four glazed donuts and four milks and cereals. When she returned to the cool room, she found Romero still sleeping comfortably. She went over to the table where she placed the breakfast and sat before the laptop. When she touched the mouse sensor, her email page appeared. Juliet could see seventeen new messages in her inbox. She was surprised and thought to wake Romero but she decided to let him rest. Just until she read a few emails. Clicking on the first one it read:

To: Sweet Baby

From: Hunk64

Message:

    i saw your ad on craigs. i think your beautiful. i stay in LA but i'll be in long beach in two days for work. i would love to wine and dine you. i can also tame that wild side of yours. call my cell at...

Juliet clicked on the next and it read:

To: Sweet Baby

From: Mr. Sunshine State

Message:

    Liked your ad. I live in town and would love to do the nasty. Pick the restaurant and the menu's all yours. Call me at...

Juliet was happy and disgusted at the same time. Romero was right, guys were so weak when it came to wanting a young girl to lay with. She figured that was why her own father did what he did. Juliet wondered if he cared that she was gone. She wondered if he alerted the police about her disappearance. Tossing the thought from her mind, Juliet went over and crawled on the bed over to Romero. She smiled as she pulled the covers down off his head. He was snoring lightly when she bent over and kissed him tenderly on his closed right eyelid. He stirred.

"Romey, baby... Baby we got some hits," she told him soft and sweet in his ear.

"Huh?" he said groggily. "What?"

"I said we got some hits. Seventeen emails."

Romero heard her clearly that time and he popped upright.

"Seventeen?" he said in disbelief as Juliet sat beside him, grinning proudly. "Get the fuck outta here."

"My word. Seventeen emails, go check," she told him.

"Hand me them boxers down there," he told her, tossing the covers off his naked body. Once he slipped his boxers on, Romero went and sat in front of the computer. When he touched the mousepad, he was shocked to see the seventeen emails in the inbox. He instantly began to read through them all. Juliet stood at his side, reading the rest of the emails. All the messages were from men wanting to meet, and all but one contacted her through Facebook.

"Damn, lil' mama... you got these dudes ready to eat you up. Did you read these already?"

"Just two. Do you want me to pour your milk on your cereal before it gets warm? I took four donuts this time, and four cereals. I figured we might need to eat the rest later on," she said to him.

"Go 'head and pour it for me," he told her, never taking his eyes off the screen. "All these studs sound white too."

"Good, cause white people have money," she stated.

"You ain't lyin', and they gon' pay to play too. I'm finna put a spiel together for you cause we need to call these studs and set up some appointments."

Juliet brought him his bowl of cereal and stood at his side once again. "Do I get to choose who I want?" she asked.

"Mhmm, yeah, go 'head. Choose how many you feel you can handle too," he told her, taking a bite out of one of the glazed donuts. As he ate, Juliet looked over the potential client list, only seven men posted pictures with their messages but she chose a couple of men who looked "well off." She also chose the man from Facebook. In total she picked three guys, all in the local area. From there, after Romero finished his breakfast and took care of his morning functions, he put together a "call spiel" for Juliet. Once he had what he needed to be said, he ran over it with her a few times before the real call. Then, when he felt she was ready, he made the call to the first man. Juliet was nervous as she listened as the phone rang twice before picking up.

"Hello?" the man said on the other line.

"Uh..." she said, looking to Romero who stood in front of her. "Is this Jerry?"

"This is Jerry, who's this?"

"This is Sweet Baby... you emailed me."

"Oh, hello, what's up sweetness?" he said, chipper.

"Hey, um... I was calling to take you up on that offer, but I was thinking we skip dinner and go straight for dessert back at my motel." These was a pause on the line and Juliet shrugged to Romero. Then the man came back on.

"That sounds good, what do I need to bring?"

"What do you need to bring?" she said, looking to Romero who nodded her on. "Just your wallet for... the sweet ice cream."

"Sounds good. Where are you? What time should I swing by?" Jerry asked.

"The Lucky Nights Inn down on Fuller and Windlow. Room 29. Can you be here in twenty minutes?"

"The Lucky Nights Inn on Fuller and Windglow?" he asked.

"On Fuller and Windlow, room 29," she repeated.

"Twenty minutes it is, Sweet Baby."

"All right, I'll be here," she said as she hung up the phone. Juliet blew out hot air with wide eyes. She had done it, she had really made a date.

"You all good, Jay?" Romero asked her. He could see that she looked nervous a bit.

"Yeah, I'm fine. It's just... really real now," she told him, flopping back onto the bed.

"He's on the way, right?"

"Twenty minutes."

"And you ready for this?" he asked.

"Yeah, ready as I ever will be."

"Aight, well... put your hair into two pigtails while I make this room look presentable. We got us some company comin'."

* * *

Sandra McNeil smiled brightly as she inhaled the fresh West Coast air. She had been on the road for days but she had finally arrived. The bus station was packed with travelers from all walks of life. Whites, blacks, Asians, Hispanics; all were in attendance as they loaded and unloaded onto their buses. The first thing she did was purchase a newspaper. When she had the time to chill out she would job search. Sandra saw that she was downtown so she just began to walk and sightsee. Making her way down Lancer Street, she marveled at the fancy cars and skyscrapers. She couldn't keep her eyes focused, like a child in a toy store she was overwhelmed. Sandra walked the city for over two hours before stopping at a McDonalds to fill her empty stomach. Ordering a large meal, she sat by the window so she could continue to view the city. Sandra looked through the newspaper at the want ads but wasn't qualified for the high-paying jobs, fast food seemed like the only option but she didn't want a regular 9 to 5, she wanted to be a star. Then, at the bottom of the page, she read an advertisement for a photo agency. The company was called Pro-Shop Photography and the ad said they "specialized in professional stills for rising movie stars and models." It was just what she needed to get her face and name out there. She pulled out her phone and placed the information of the company inside it. When she was done eating she would call and find out more details. Sandra thought about her mom and stepdad. She wondered if they called missing persons or did they even care that she had left? If she had to guess… her stepdad would be relieved that she wasn't his problem anymore, and her mother would only care once she was sober enough to actually feel any compassion.

After a fine meal, Sandra neglected to call the photo agency and headed for the beach. She had asked a cute couple who were also dining at the time where it was located. It just so happened that the young couple had just come from there and had come to eat lunch. Sandra took the four-block walk to Long Beach and when she got there she was flabbergasted. She had never seen so many people in one place before. She was from the state of Maine where the only action is fishing for seafood.

Sandra weaved her way through the crowded sands, watching people play volleyball, Frisbee, and tag. She smiled as three little kids chased one another with squirt guns. Finally she found a spot, dropped her bags and pulled out a dry towel from back home. She was dressed in shorts and a t-shirt so she didn't feel too overdressed. She needed a full-body tan but she didn't have a bathing suit so she simply laid under the bright sun allowing her exposed body parts to bronze. Now this is heaven, she smiled with closed eyes. She had to find a place to sleep tonight, she pondered. It has to be cheap because money is precious, she thought. Tomorrow I'll go get my picture taken, but today… today I relax.

Chapter 5

"Remember what I told you, Juliet. Tell the chump to show you his 'joint.' If he don't pull it out and show you... then he a police and you need to shut shit down and play the dummy role, but if he do... come into the bathroom and I'll take care of the rest, feel me?" Romero was running over the plan once more. He would hide in the bathroom until she asked the "trick" to show his dick, and if he did she would come get him and he would speak with the guy one-on-one to let him know it was business and it was governed by a boss who would keep an eye out for his girl. Juliet was surprisingly calm. She had butterflies in her belly but now she was ready. Ready to make money to please her new man.

"I understand, Romey," she told him. She was dressed in a short, blue jean skirt, thin silken white blouse, and no footwear or socks. Her hair was pulled into two pigtails that dangled to the back, lip-balm-covered lips, and skin that glowed milky white with a baby lotion fragrance. Romero admitted she looked cute, about 14 fourteen years old but cute... and that's what he wanted. Moments later there came a knock at the door. They looked at each other with knowing.

"Come here," Romero told her, extending his neck and giving her a peck to the lips. "Go be my star."

Juliet smiled as he went into the bathroom. She went to the door and took a deep breath.

"Yes?" she called to the person on the other side of the door.

"It's Jerry," the voice said low. When Juliet opened the door, the summer heat and bright sunlight rushed in. Out on the motel's walkway stood the man known as Jerry. He was about thirty- to thirty-five-years-old looking, with thick, square glasses, thin, wet black hair that was laid down and parted, and looked like a high school science teacher. He wore a plaid short-sleeve dress shirt with brown Carhartt work pants and brown penny loafers. In his hand he held a bag from the 7-Eleven up the block and it had a tub of ice cream inside. Juliet computed the man's overall visual assessment and within those milliseconds she told herself, "He's geeky but not fat and nasty. I can do him."

"Hey, come on in," she told him, stepping to the side. Jerry came inside and stood awkwardly as she closed the door behind him.

"I brought the dessert," he said, holding the ice cream out to her.

"Ah, thank you," she said, taking it with a smile. "Come on in and sit down."

Jerry came in and took a seat at the table. There was some left over ice in the room bucket that Romero had got earlier in the day so Juliet put the tub of ice cream in it. She then came and sat across from Jerry.

"Did you find me okay?" she asked, making small talk.

"Oh yeah, my GPS got me here," he told her, nodding.

"Good... So, Jerry... let me ask you a question."

"All right," he said.

"Are you single?"

"Yes, very."

"Does it bother you that I'm just seventeen?" she asked.

"Well... age is just a number, some would say."

"And what do you say?"

"Well... I'd have to agree," he told her.

"Jerry, are you a cop?" she boldly asked. He frowned and shifted uncomfortably.

"Cop? No, why ask that?" he asked her, puzzled.

"Because I wanna fuck, and I'm only seventeen, and I wanna know if you're gonna try and bust me or something. So, are you a cop?" Jerry was caught off guard but he was also glad to hear the female speak of having sex with him. This is what he came for.

"I'm no cop, Sweet Baby. Are you a cop or undercover?" he asked right back. This was it, Juliet thought.

"Let's do a little show and tell. Pull your cock out and show me it and I'll spread my legs so you can see my cotton panties." There came a pause between them. Jerry was extremely aroused by the sexual nature of their conversation. He wanted to see those panties.

"All right, but you're next," he said, unbuttoning and zipping down his pants. Seconds later, Juliet was looking at his "piece." He was no cop.

"See, there it is, nice and hard," he said to her, wiggling himself back and forth.

"Okay, well, a deal's a deal," she told him uncrossing her legs and sat with open legs. Jerry tilted his head to get a better view and when he did he saw her panties which were white with red polka dots on them.

"Oh yeah, that's hot, lil' polka dots, huh?" he said with hungry eyes. He stroked his manhood lightly as he looked on.

"That's enough of that for now," she said, closing her legs and standing up. "Put that monster up for now. I'll be right back, I have to use the restroom. Make yourself comfortable, turn on the TV." Juliet went into the restroom and Romero stood waiting. They said nothing to each other, they just switched locations. When he came out, closing the door behind him, he found Jerry standing with his back turned; he was fixing his pants. Romero stood in the middle of the room with his hands crossed behind his back.

"Today is yo' lucky day," Romero said to him. The male voice shook Jerry's core and he twisted around quick, startled.

"Whoa, don't panic, boss, everything's still all good," Romero assured him with halted hands and a smirk.

"Who are you?" Jerry asked, not only puzzled but a bit nervous now.

"I'm the broker, call me Rome. Look, you and I know why you're here, you came to get some young tail. I understand so don't be coy. Check it… Sweet Baby is willing to do the nasty but it cost to play. This what I need and this what I need you to know. First off, be nice to my girl, she's yours but only for a moment. She comes to you in one piece and she needs to come back to me the same way. Next thing, safety first, no Jimmy-hat no kitty-cat. Third, this is a low-key, private party in which you can swing by whenever you set up a date, just email her and wait till she hit you back. Lastly, pay what's agreed to, don't get cheap and try to bargain… this is pussy and not a garage sale. Now… do you understand all of what I said before I leave you two kids alone?" Romero's speech was perfect, just the way he rehearsed. Jerry stood stunned. He didn't see this coming, he wanted to run out of there but he was in too deep, plus he really wanted to have sex with the girl in the bathroom. The guy—Rome—was straight with him and seemed okay. Jerry went for it.

"Nope, I completely understand," he told Romero.

"Good," he said, turning and going back to the bathroom. He knocked twice on the door and kept moving until he reached the front door and left. Moments later, Juliet emerged from the bathroom dressed in nothing but a small t-shirt and her panties. She came walking slowly over to Jerry whose eyes were locked on hers.

"Well that was a surprise," he said to her in a flat tone.

"Don't take it personal. So, Jerry… tell me what nasty things you wanna do with Sweet Baby," she said to him. Juliet's deep green eyes seemed to cast a spell over him and he once again became aroused.

"Uh… well, what—uh… what do you do? What's your price?"

"For you? Twenty for my hands, fifty for my mouth, a hundred for this sweet pussy, or one-fifty for the full package. What'll it be… Jerry?" she said seductively. Jerry's loins burned—he was horny as a dog in heat.

"Um… wow, huh… I uh…" He was shy. Juliet reached out and grabbed his hard-on. Jerry gasped with pleasure and his heart began to race.

"Don't be shy, honey, tell me what you want," she said to him, looking up into his face.

"I want you… I want to bury my face in your sweet, tight ass," he finally told her. Juliet was shocked but didn't show it, she just kept playing her role.

"Oh, is that right? Is that what you want to do? And what about my king-size down here? Does he wanna play?"

"Oh, he wants to play," Jerry told her. Juliet took him by the hand and let him test the firmness of her small breast. It felt nice when his fingers rubbed over her hardened nipples. She next led him to the bed where she told him to take his pants off. She got completely naked and laid flat on her stomach. She rested her head on her hands and looked sideways at him in her peripheral view.

"Put that face in my ass," she told him softly. Jerry could hardly contain himself as he struggled a bit to get his pants off his ankles. Once he did he climbed on the bed behind Juliet and as if in a pie-eating contest he buried his nose and mouth into the crack of Juliet's white ass. Juliet's toes curled and her mouth fell slightly ajar as the surge of pleasure shot through her body. Jerry held each butt cheek and licked wildly at her pussy and asshole. Juliet arched her butt up into his face even more as it felt so good. She could take it like that all night. When Jerry stopped he was ready for sex but pulled a condom from his wallet. He remembered what the guy told him beforehand. Slipping on the condom, Jerry returned to Juliet, still flat on her stomach. He mounted her and guided his throbbing cock into the opening of her wet cunt.

"Ooo, there it is, there's that dick, you gonna fuck this tight little pussy? You gonna give it to Sweet Baby?" Juliet spoke dirty because it was one of the keys Romero had given her, men loved to be talked to and praised during sex.

"You just wait and see, you little fox you," he told her. Jerry pushed himself deep inside her and groaned. Then, while in his mounted push-up position, he began to pump slow, then faster with more force. Juliet gripped the sheets with both hands as she was taken from behind, her body jerked with every thrust and she couldn't help but to moan out. She was having sex with a stranger for money now, this was the real deal... and it felt so right.

"Oooh Jerry... Jerry, your cock is so deep, God you're gonna make me come, you're gonna make Sweet Baby come all on your cock," she moaned and cried. Juliet was using the keys she was given by Romero but she was also telling half truth. Jerry was deep, deep, and hitting her spot. Jerry could take no more and started to speed up more, he was about to bust. Seconds later, with a loud, angry grunt, he came hard into the condom inside her. Out of breath and overworked, Jerry stood up and began to pull his clothes back on. Juliet rolled over and sat with crossed legs on the edge of the head of the bed. She smiled warmly at him as he slipped on his pants and shoes.

"Let's make it a flat one hundred, let's not tell my man I didn't charge you for that first part," she told him.

Going inside his wallet, Jerry counted out a hundred bucks in tens and twenties. He tried to hand it to her but she pointed to the nightstand. "Let's not make this the last time, Jerry. You'll have a sure thing with me," she told him.

"Oh, I'll be reaching out again, Sweet Baby, trust me. I get paid in a week, I'll email you then," he explained.

When Jerry left out the room, Juliet retired to the shower as she was told to do after each session. Downstairs, outside, Romero stood by a tree just beyond the motel's parking lot. He was speaking long distance to his mother on his cell phone. He was telling her what she wanted to hear when he saw Jerry "the Nerd" come out of his room. He watched as he got into a new-looking Ford pickup truck. Romero headed back over to the motel, wrapping up the conversation with his mama. When he made it upstairs and came into the room, he heard the shower running. The atmosphere smelled like musky sex as he rounded the corner and saw the neatly stacked cash on the nightstand. He picked it up, counted it and nodded with a smile. A hundred dollars, quick! Even though he was a long way off from what he lost, he knew he could make it back if he pushed Juliet onto more clients. He pocketed the cash and pulled his laptop out from under the bed. He then went over to the table and turned on its power. Five minutes later Juliet emerged in a towel wrapped tightly around her body, her wet hair hung down her back. She came over to Romero who was sitting behind his computer and gave him a hug around the neck.

"You got the money?" she asked, already knowing.

"Yeah, thank you. How was it?" he asked, logging on to her email account.

"It was nothing. Easy, quick... nobody is better than you, Romey," she told him, kissing his cheek. "What are you doing now? Booking another one?" she asked, going over to the bed and sitting down.

"I'm finna see if we got some more hits, why? Can you handle another one?" he asked.

"I mean... yeah, we need more than a hundred dollars."

"Aight, well... get the list you chose and make the call. Just remember the spiel."

Juliet pulled the list from the nightstand drawer and picked up the phone. She dialed the number for a man who called himself "Hot Six-Pack." While she made her calls, Romero found three more emails and over thirty friend requests on Facebook. He was thrilled, all the guys looked like potential tricks who would pay for pussy. Some were even in their 40s.

"Mr. Wonderful," Romero read to himself. "Hey there, Sweet Baby. I'd like to show you a night out on the town. You and I can go up the coast in my Bentley coupe and eat some fresh-caught crab at Chez Marie. After that we can walk on the beach and drink white wine as the sun sets. You need a tamer for your wild side? Well, I'll bring my whip and we can do some really nasty things. Call me at this number." Romero liked the client's style but wasn't sure he was telling the truth. Online a person could be whoever they wanted with billions in the bank, but when you finally came face to face with that person, they could be broke down and poor. Romero read a few more.

"All right sweetie… Uh huh, see you then… bye-bye," Juliet ended her third call and came over to Romero and hugged him around the neck again. "All set, babe."

"What up?" he asked.

"I booked three more."

"Three?! You booked three more? When? For when?" he asked, shocked. Juliet went over to her bag and pulled out more clothes.

"For today and tonight. One of the guys is coming in a half hour, the next at four o'clock, and the last at seven because that's when he gets off work.

Romero looked at his cell phone and saw that it was 1:40 p.m., the guy would be there in twenty minutes. He was surprised at Juliet but was happy to see she seemed to fall right into the "hoe groove." He had to start speaking more like a boss pimp.

"That's what I like to see," he turned halfway in his chair. "Teamwork. You my number two. I'm king, you queen."

Juliet smiled at him but said nothing. She knew what he was doing or thought he was doing. He was boosting her ego. She knew he was using her to get money just as her father was using her body when she was younger. Difference was, Juliet didn't want to do the things her father made her do, she wanted to do the things she could for Romero. She somehow loved him already. He was a boy who showed kindness and wanted to see her taken care of. But she would hold the "L-word" to herself for a while, guys seemed to run away from that word and she didn't want to lose him. As Romero went back to the computer, she slipped back into her panties and the same outfit, only this time she put on socks and prepared an outfit for later on. She needed more clothes, sexy undergarments like Victoria's Secret, so she could really entice her clients.

"We got some more fish on the hooks," Romero told her, closing down the computer's top. "But we'll get to them later on. Right now 'm finna get ready for yo' next dude to roll through." He got up out of the chair with computer in hand, came over to the bed and slid it under. He stood before Juliet and thought to himself, "Damn… I got one."

"What?" she said, looking up at him.

"Nothing… Just looking at a star," he told her. Juliet blushed with a frown. He was boosting again but she wanted to hear more.

"Please," she said to him sarcastically.

"Please? Please nothing, lil' mama. Look, you a star, point blank, period. You shine bright for me and I dig that about you. We gon' go to the top, I promise. With me behind the wheel and you in the passenger seat… ain't no stopping us. You my bitch and 'm yo' nigga, we a mufuckin' team, I told you," Romero said with conviction. Juliet shook her head up and down.

"Aight then, know that 100%." He bent down and tilted her chin with his index finger and kissed her lightly on the lips. "And when we reach the top… when I make my first hundred thousand… 'm gonna take you anywhere on earth you wanna go. Where you wanna go, lil' mama?"

She thought to herself for a moment, then it came to her.

"New York City, but it could be anywhere as long as I'm with you," she told him.

Romero smiled and was flattered. "New York it is then, and we'll sleep like royalty at the muthafuckin' Waldorf Astoria," Romero told her, laying another kiss on her lips. This time it went deeper and deeper until he was slowly falling on top of her with his hands all on her breasts, but moment into it there came a knock at the front door. Romero looked at his watch and it was two o'clock. He looked down into Juliet's eyes and said, "You ready to make some bread?"

She nodded. "Yes."

Chapter 6

It was almost checkout time at the Best Western motel on Edison Avenue when Sandra was putting the finishing touches on her makeup. The day before she had chilled at the beach almost all day just catching sun and snacking on boardwalk food. Eventually she ended up purchasing a cheap bathing suit from one of the many beachfront shops and went swimming in the cool ocean. After that she took a city bus to a motel not too far away. When Sandra checked in, she paid $50 and went up to her room where she found it to be comfortable and clean. That night, she had received several calls from her parents and she simply told them that she was "fine" and "finding her own way." After several attempts to get her to reconsider coming back home or even reveal her location, Sandra simply hung up and shut her phone off all together.

Just as she had promised herself, Sandra had called and scheduled an appointment at Pro-Shop Photography. She had to be there by one o'clock but she needed to head out sooner because she needed to take a cab the unknown distance. She didn't know exactly how far it was but seeing the "East" on the address when she knew she was out south… a cab had to be called. When she was done painting her face, she stood looking in the bathroom mirror. She felt she looked good. She was 5'9", slender from top to bottom, with a bronze complexion naturally because of her grandparents' Native American roots. Her hair was long and dark, her eyes a greenish hazel, lips full like Angelina Jolie, boobs like Taylor Swift, and a butt like the average model type. All in all she was considered pretty by the guys back East who always told her she could be a model. Sandra didn't pay the boys much mind because they'd tell a girl anything to get in her pants, but she did listen to the praises of her few girl friends who told her she should leave town and go to Hollywood. Long Beach wasn't quite Hollywood, but it was close enough. She'd get there eventually.

When the taxi picked her up in the motel lot, they headed east. Once they finally arrived, the fare was over twenty dollars. Entering the building which was located downtown on a highly populated strip, she carried her bags to the front desk where she was greeted by a female clerk wearing a short, bobbed red wig.

"Hello, welcome to Pro-Shop Studio, how may I help you?"

"My name is Sandra McNeil, I have an appointment at one p.m.," she told the clerk with a smile.

The redhead checked her paperwork and nodded with a smile of confirmation. She then reached into the desk and pull out an application sheet and pen.

"Fill this out to the best of your knowledge, return it to me, and we'll get you back to the studio," the clerk told her. Sandra took the clipboard, lugged her things over to the waiting area and took a seat. As she filled the paperwork out she looked around the front lobby and saw many framed photos of celebrities who seemingly took headshots at the studio. The list went from Sean Penn to Michael Douglas on down to Ashley Judd and Kate Hudson. As she looked, a woman emerged from the back of the studio. She was tall, thin, and beautiful. She was dressed in a black and white pencil skirt that looked to be from a top-notch designer, and she walked with an air of snobbism in her nice heels as she left out the front door into the sunny summer day. The desk clerk noticed Sandra looking and smiled at the fact. She had seen the look many times, it was intimidation.

"That was the woman from all those sexy Fiat 500 commercials. She's such a prude. You're much prettier."

"I don't know about that but thank you," Sandra blushed, turning her attention back to the application.

"Hey," the clerk said. "Don't sell yourself short. I've seen girls come and go, be confident and fierce… you never know what's out there for you."

Sandra smiled at her warmly as she came over and handed her the clipboard and pen. The clerk scanned it fast and pushed a call button. A moment later, a voice came over and the clerk told the voice, "Sandra McNeil, for her one o'clock." The voice told her to bring her back so the clerk waved her to follow until they reached a door that read "Studio Room B. Keep door closed." When they entered, Sandra saw a wide open space filled with backdrops, props, lights, wires, and all types of photography stuff. Right at the door was a desk and chair with a woman sitting behind it, finger-scrolling through a computer tablet. The desk clerk led the way and handed the clipboard to the woman who took it before she turned and left.

"Hello," the woman said with a British accent as she stood up and presented her hand. "You must be Ms. McNeil."

"Yes, we spoke on the phone," she told her, taking her hand.

"Please, have a seat and let's see what Pro-Shop can help you with."

*   *   *

As the motel air conditioner pumped cold air with a steady low hum, Romero sat at the table counting his cash. Juliet lay bundled up in the blanket asleep on the bed. She deserved to have her rest after the gamut she ran on the three clients from the previous night. It was a wild thing being a pimp. Even though Romero didn't like the word when it came to him it was the truth, he indeed was pushing a woman onto men for sex for money in return. Juliet, as young as she was, laid it down like a seasoned vet. She put her body to work and somehow raked in over $900 in total. The guys she "sexed" didn't have a problem opening their wallets as long as she opened her mouth and legs. When the night was done and the last man had gone back to his normal life... Romero took Juliet into the shower and bathed her like she was literally a queen. He washed her from feet to face, taking care to wash her entire body without her help. He wanted to show her he cared. He needed to show her that he still valued her even after she had sex with strange men. And she loved it. Never in her life had she had a man wash her clean and do it with such care. Juliet was tired and finished but she could have went more rounds for the money, but Romero told her that her "coochie shop" was closed for the night. She couldn't lie but she was proud of the money she had made for Romero. Seeing how he lit up when he came in and saw the money on the nightstand, how he congratulated her on a job well done when she emerged out of the bathroom from the shower... it made her want to keep going.

Romero checked the computer and did morning research on the sites and wrote down more potential clients who left phone numbers. Just that fast the business of selling pussy was booming. He had a plan, but first he wanted to do something for his young star to keep her on the team... and willing.

So Romero quietly slipped on some clothes and left. He went out into the sunny warm morning and walked with haste up Wilmont Street and across Vandermill Avenue until he reached a small neighborhood store he had seen called Rubeco's Urban Closet. Romero came in and asked one of the black female workers to assist him in picking out a nice outfit for a young lady Juliet's size. The store worker whose name was Cassandra took him to the women's section and put together a nice outfit, an outfit that consisted of a black V-neck cotton tee, dark blue stretch leggings, and a pair of inexpensive four-inch matching black heels by Forever 21. The bill was $45 once he hit the shop next door called Dots and bought her a few matching sets of bras and panties. After that he stopped by a local florist shop and purchased a half-dozen pink roses. When Romero got back to the motel and back into the room, he found Juliet still balled up under the covers. He came over and got on the bed with gifts in hand, pulled the blanket from over her and kissed her on the side of the mouth. Juliet stirred, opening her eyes a bit. She didn't see the gifts because he was still close to her face.

"Mmm… babe," she shyly said, turning her face into the pillow. "I have morning breath."

"Give me them lips, fuck some morning breath," he told her with passion. Juliet instantly turned her head back to him and did as she was told, and they kissed softly. "Wake up, yo' man went out and got you something," he told her, standing upright on the side of the bed. Juliet's eyes opened with a squint and she sat up. She smiled wide as she was handed her flowers and shopping bag.

"Ooh, Romey, thank you," she swooned while putting her nose in the flower petals. She set them down and pulled the clothes and heels from the bag.

"Ooh, Romey, these are cute," she said, admiring the heels. "This outfit is so nice… you didn't have to buy me anything."

"Baby, as long as you my bitch, you gon' look shitty-sharp. That lil' shit ain't nothing really, just wait till the bread really start to flip, you gon' look like a movie star. Now go on 'head and take care of yo' morning hygiene and put that shit on, we finna go eat some breakfast down at IHOP.

Juliet tossed away the blanket and went to the bathroom. She was happy to get out in public with her man, especially in a new outfit. While she took care of herself, Romero checked the email and nothing had changed. There were still a couple of unread ones but he would get to those later. Juliet came out of the bathroom minutes later fully dressed and looked good. Romero nodded while rubbing his hands together, he liked what she was invoking inside him because if she looked sexy to him… she looked sexy to most.

"How do I look? I haven't worn many heels," she said with folded hands in front of her. She had put water in her hair and brushed it, it was now pulled tightly to the back in a braided tail. Her perky breasts pressed against the cotton tee just right and the leggings hugged the lower half of her body perfectly. Her cute toes peeking through the tips of the heels were unpedicured but fine. Romero wanted to pat himself on the back.

"Baby, you look fine as a box of wine. Mm-mm-mm, twirl around for me so I can see how that lil' butt workin'," he told her. Juliet turned around and showed him while looking over her shoulder. Her firm backside sat up nicely as well.

"Mmm! Damn, can you bend over the bed right fast and let me get a quick nut off?" he asked, joking.

Juliet smacked her lips, rolling her eyes. She slid her thumbs in the waistband of her leggings and began to push them to the floor.

"'m just playin', 'm just playin'," Romero said, stopping her. "We finna go eat."

"Babe... don't do me like that, you know I love it when you tell me you wanna have sex," she said to him.

Romero came over to her and smacked her lightly on the butt and kissed her glossy lips.

"Come on, 'm hungry," he said, heading for the door.

*   *   *

It was around eleven o'clock when Romero and Juliet finished their meals at the IHOP down on Sherman Street. They both ate pancakes, eggs, sausage links, and drank orange juice. They sat in a corner booth by the window, looking out at the busy city. Romero had been in deep thought about a plan.

"Lil' mama," he called softly. "Tell me your life's dream."

Juliet sipped on her drink and shrugged. She didn't really know how to answer... no one had ever asked her such a serious question before.

"Umm... well, I don't really have many talents. I can't sing or dance well. I can't write books or anything. I barely finished high school... I don't know. I have always dreamed of having a family of my own one day, maybe have two kids, be a stay-at-home mom."

Romero nodded, returning her warm smile.

"Housewife, huh?"

"Mhmm. What about you?"

"Me? I told you, on top, making enough money to live comfortable for the rest of my life."

"Do you want kids?" she asked, hopeful.

"Shorties? …Yeah, I can see myself with a lil' Romero runnin' round the crib, why? You want me to pop a lil' one in you?" he asked calmly.

Juliet blushed. "It doesn't matter what I want. It's up to you, you're the king, remember?"

"Yeah, well… who knows… let's make this money first before we start making babies. Speaking of money… I've been thinking, we should make this thing we got goin' more professional, more exclusive."

"Like how?" she asked, curious.

"Aight, hear me out… Look, back in the city, the guys in my hood sell dope. Their bags are their calling cards and the smokers know who to call when it's time to buy the best. This thing we got going on is the same thing. So I'm thinking I go online to Vistaprint, it's a company that makes flyers and cards for super cheap. Go there, print up some calling cards and when they come… hand them shits out to the clients we feel got bank."

Juliet liked his idea. She knew if clients had the card on them, like in their wallets, then it would be a constant reminder every time they saw it, a reminder of her and what she could do to make them feel good. The card would symbolize two things: pussy for them, and money for her to give to her man.

"Babe, I like it but whose number's gonna be on the card?" she asked.

"Good question, check this… 'm gonna buy another celly just for the clients. The only time that phone gonna ring is for money. And it's gonna be one of them over-the-counter cheap Tracfones so we don't have to have no mans on it, feel me?"

"All right, sounds good, when we gonna do all this?" she asked, anxious to get started. He looked at the time.

"Shiiit… we can go snatch a celly up now and head back to the tip right after. Vistaprint got 48-hour service delivery," he explained as he pulled two dollars from his billfold and placed it as the tip on the table.

After picking up the prepaid phone from Walmart, they took the bus back to the motel. When they got back in, Romero instantly went online to Vistaprint.com and started brainstorming. He knew exactly what he wanted which was a standard size business card, solid black background, premium gloss lamination, with a graphic lip print on the other side. Simple, but with the exclusiveness of a million dollar black card. The website required a credit card but Romero called their customer service line and setup other means of payment which was sending a money order overnight delivery. He went across the street to the gas station and got the $35 money order and from there went three blocks over to the post office and sent it off. When he came out of the heat back into the cool comfort of his room and found Juliet on the computer, she was live chatting with a man by email.

"Babe, babe, I'm talking to a guy right now who seems loaded. He says he wants to drive me up the coast in his Bentley coupe!" Juliet reported happily.

"Oh yeah?" Romero said, kicking off his shoes and tossing off his hot t-shirt. "Is his name Mr. Wonderful?"

"Yeah, how'd you know?" she asked, puzzled.

"Because I read his email this morning. What he talkin' 'bout? He wanna spend some money?" Romero didn't have to tell her to get up, she just did. When he sat down, he pulled her onto his lap. He read the last message sent by Mr. Wonderful.

"Are you really only seventeen?"

Romero answered as Juliet. "Yes... but... I'm... emancipated. Is... that a... problem?"

Pause.

"Not at all, I'm almost fifty and I feel like I'm still in my twenties. Personal question."

Romero shook his head. He could see from the way the conversation was going that Mr. Wonderful was going to ask some freakish stuff. So he answered, "Ask away."

There was the pause.

"Are you a virgin?" Mr. Wonderful emailed.

Romero scoffed, looking up to Juliet.

"Baby, we got another one," he told her before responding back.

"Let's... just say... I have... experienced... my share of... sexual... encounters."

Pause.

"Oh really? You sound like a bad girl. Have you tried oral sex in those encounters?"

"No... but I'm always... up for... new things." Romero paused for a moment before he typed the last words. "If the guy and price is right."

Pause.

"Businesswoman. I like your style. It's a good thing I'm well off... and well hung. Wink-wink."

Romero and Juliet snickered to themselves at his perverted last comment. Mr. Wonderful was on the hook.

"Mmm... sounds tasty... how 'bout... you swing by... my motel room... and we can... see if I can... make your wink-wink disappear down my throat." Romero looked to Juliet before sending it and she nodded with a confirming smile.

Pause.

"Location and time?" emailed Mr. Wonderful.

"The Lucky Nights Inn... on the east side... room 29."

"What should I bring, besides myself?" he emailed.

"Besides your big cock? Just your big wallet."

Pause.

"Give me about an hour-thirty. I have a meeting to attend to but it'll be quick. See you soon, Sweet Baby."

"I'll be waiting. Bye-bye." Romero logged off and closed down the computer. He took a deep breath and looked up into Juliet's face. She was smiling down at him.

"Whatchu think?" he asked, rubbing her back softly.

"I don't think, I just do for you," she said nonchalantly.

Romero frowned. "Why you say it like that, lil' mama?" he asked, perplexed.

"Babe... you got me, you don't need to always ask me if I'm good with a guy. If you want me to do something or somebody, then just say it... and I'll do it," she told him, plain and simple.

Shit, Romero thought, this chick wanted to be bossed. She wanted him to basically stop being so soft and direct her without asking her opinion.

He had to make sure though.

"Aight lil' mama, I hear you. I just be tryna see if you be good, but since I see you is and you stay ready... I gotchu now. So hear this... when buddy roll through and I lay the game down... 'm gonna need you to work extra hard on him, get his ass to show you how much money he brought in his wallet, and if it's fat! We need all of it."

"All of it?" she said, moving her head back with confusion.

"All of it, he repeated.

"Romey what if—"

"You got the power, lil' mama," he cut in sternly. "You my bitch... use them keys I gave you. The man say he well off so the lil' money he gon' have in his wallet is like pocket change. Play the role. Now, tell yo' nigga what you gon' do."

Juliet froze for a moment. She didn't want to fail him after speaking to him like she was a go-bot who could do anything she was told, but what he was asking might be too much. She sighed, kissed him on the temple and told him, "'mma get all his money."

"That's what I like to hear," he said proudly. "Now take care of ya man real quick."

"Whatchu want?" she asked down to him.

"What you will never give a trick. Yo' real love."

Juliet smiled warmly and agreed with him in her mind. "So what you want, babe?" she asked again.

"Hmm," he said, tapping her to get off him. She stood to the side of him and watched as he turned the chair outward. "I first want you to get naked. Then, 'mma pull dick out and I want you to sit on it."

Juliet smiled. "All right," she said, turning and pushing her leggings to the floor.

Chapter 7

"Sandra McNeil!" the heavyset woman from the backroom called. She had been called into a commercial casting as an extra in an Old Navy promotion. Thing was, there were over fifty other girls who showed up. Sandra had taken her headshots at Pro-Shop Photography and also bought their temporary management package. The management package basically shopped her name around California to any castings looking for females of her type, and when a casting came up she would receive a call telling her where she could show up, for what, and the time and date. Even though it cost her $50 she felt it was necessary if she wanted to get noticed by the right people. The bad part was it put a large hole in her funds, leaving her with nothing more than $300 or so.

"That's me," she said, standing up and going back. When she entered the room, she was faced with three people who sat behind a single table. Two women and a man. They all looked bored and expressionless. The fat woman who called her in told her to stand on an X that was taped to the carpet. There was a cameraman ready to film her. She was beyond nervous.

"Okay, Ms. McNeil, we've looked over your Pro-Shop package and we assume you know why you're here. This role only has a few extras echoing the main actress and only requires a couple of lines. I will give you the lines and we'll go over the skit several times on camera and you can be on your way. Alrighty?" the man in the middle told her.

"Yes, understood," she nodded with a smile. The casting director picked up a sheet of paper and began to read from it.

"Ms. McNeil, your lines are: 'Wow! These Old Navy jeans are the best,' and you'll say it with sex appeal but be posh. When I say my line, I'll point at you and you'll go. Understand?" he asked.

"Understood."

"All right... Wow, these Old Navy jeans are the best." He pointed to Sandra.

"wow... Um... these Old Navy jeans are awesome," she said with a bright smile. She knew she botched the line.

"All right, let's stick with the lines this time, okay?"

55

"Okay."

"All right… wow, these Old Navy jeans are the best." He once again pointed to Sandra.

"Wow! These jeans from Old Navy are the best," she said with another bright smile. Damn it! she thought. Messed up again.

The casting director cleared his throat and stacked some paper in front of him.

"Well, close enough. Ms. McNeil, thank you, you may go. If you are chosen then you'll be contacted through your management rep at Pro-Shop."

The fat woman who escorted her in opened the door for her to exit. Sandra waved awkwardly to the three casting directors but only received smug looks in return. When Sandra stepped out of the building the day was at its end and the sun was golden orange as it began its descent under the horizon. She had been waiting in line all afternoon and now she was caught across town after dark, miles away from her motel and hungry. Sandra didn't want to take another cab but she had to. So she called the cab service and waited twenty minutes until it arrived. When it finally did, it was dark and the night was cool, too cool for her uncovered legs in her dress.

When she got back to her room she changed into a pair of jeans and a long-sleeve turtleneck with a sleeveless parka. She was hungry so she made the two-block walk over to McDonalds. Sandra walked with caution and haste down the grimy dark sidewalks of East Long Beach. She had made the walk twice before but she still wasn't comfortable being alone. She admitted it was the worst part of being away from home. About halfway to her destination she was approached from the side by a man who looked like Charles Manson. He startled her and made her flinch to the opposite direction.

"Can you spare a dollar, miss?" he asked with a zombie's walk and outstretched hands.

"Sorry, no," Sandra lied as she kept going. Her heart was racing because she was on a strip that had no lights and hardly anyone hung over there.

"You Hollywood cunts always shit on the lesser folks. Get your boney ass back here and give me a damn dollar!" the bum demanded, angry.

That was enough for Sandra. When she heard that she bolted, but as soon as she took four strides she tripped and fell hard onto the concrete sidewalk. She let out a shriek of pain as she crashed and her small clutch purse tumbled out of her grasp. Before she knew it, the dirty bum was trotting past her and snatching up her purse.

"Hah! Stupid bitch, got what you deserve... try to run from me, I wasn't even gonna do nothing," he told her frantically trying to open the purse.

Sandra sat up on her palms, watching the bum rob her. Fear was gripping her. "D-don't touch that. I'll call the police," she threatened.

"Yeah, yeah. So what, I'll be long gone by then, plus, how you gonna do that without this?" the bum held her cell phone in his hand. He then viciously smashed it on the ground. Sandra cringed as pieces of her phone zipped past her face.

"Holy hell," the bum said with amazement. He had found her folded cash. "Jackpot."

Sandra's eyes widened and her heart skipped a beat.

"No, please don't, that's all I have, mister," she pleaded.

But the bum wasn't listening, he just pocketed the cash, tossed her purse to the side, and took off running in the direction behind her.

"Sir, please!" she yelled through tears. "Sir!"

But the bum was gone. For several moments Sandra just stayed on the ground sobbing. She couldn't believe her bad luck. What was she to do now? Finally, she pulled herself together and managed to find her purse and all the things that fell out when it was thrown. Her knees hurt and so did one of her palms. She was scared to walk back to the motel because the bum ran the way she came, so she decided to continue on to McDonalds where she could sit and think about how she was going to survive off a ten dollar bill she had on the TV back at her room, and sixty-five cents left in her purse pocket.

*   *   *

"Give me two McChicken sandwiches with Big Mac sauce and cheese, a cheeseburger, two large fries with two ranch salad dressings, four apple pies, and a large Hi-C orange drink."

Juliet had volunteered to go get dinner. She pulled a twenty out of her Guess clutch purse and paid the bill. It had been three days since her big night with Mr. Wonderful and just like Romero told her to do, she got his entire billfold. Mr. Wonderful was no con man. He was well off and he did drive a Bentley. Juliet put on a show that would have made a blind man see. After Romero popped out and laid the game down on the unsuspecting creep of a gentleman, she went to work. Juliet played the young, dumb, schoolgirl role to a T and Mr. Wonderful ate it up. By the end of an hour, she had made him come twice just by jacking him off and talking dirty. She hardly sucked him off. And once he did get in her, he didn't last twenty pumps before he nutted then. Mr. Wonderful was more than happy to hand her all he had brought which was twelve hundred dollars. When she was in the shower like she always did after a session, Romero burst into the bathroom, pulled the glass doors back and stood there. Shower water spattered his clothes and the floor. Juliet thought something was wrong by the way he was looking at her but then he started to grin. He told her, "That's twelve hundred dollars."

She replied, "I didn't count it, babe."

"Bitch, you love me, don't chu?" he said, not really asking a question. And that's when she finally got the chance to tell him.

"More than myself, baby," she stated.

That same day, she serviced two more men and made four hundred more dollars, and the next day she serviced three more and made six hundred dollars. Juliet had put over $3,100 into her man's pocket and she felt on top of the world. Earlier that same day, Romero had taken her to get pampered. He bought her more clothes, including the sexy Victoria's Secret undergarments. He got her nails and toes done. He even enticed her enough to cut her hair off. He said he wanted her to have the "Emma Watson" look. She also had it dyed platinum blonde. Standing at the counter of the empty restaurant, she was dressed in an H&M miniskirt that hugged her curves. She stood 5'11" in her six-inch pumps. Two young Latino males stood behind her doing low catcalls towards her but she paid them no mind.

Tired of standing and waiting, Juliet took a seat in a corner booth and waited. As she checked her phone to see if she missed a text from Romero was when she noticed a girl about her age sitting across from her. The girl looked dazed and had tear tracks down her cheeks. Juliet being who she was instantly stuck her nose in her business and came over to her.

"Hey," Juliet said softly. "Are you all right?"

When Sandra snapped out of her zone, she looked up and saw a pretty young woman before her. She looked concerned and Sandra wiped her face and cleared her throat.

"Oh, I'm sorry, I'm… just going through something right now," she told Juliet. Sandra looked at the female's attired and wondered if she was some type of star.

"Can I sit and talk with you? Keep you company until my order is called?" Juliet asked.

"Sure… why not," Sandra told her, caring but not wanting to be alone anymore.

"Can we talk about what's bothering you? I promise not to judge," Juliet told her with sincerity. She was pretty to her, exotic even. Juliet thought she looked like Selena Gomez a small bit, only this girl's eyes were brilliant like a cat's. Juliet sat across from her with legs crossed.

"What's bothering me… well, let's see. First off, I suck at acting but it's one of my dreams. I just got robbed for the last bit of money I had by a hobo. My cell phone was destroyed. I hurt myself by tripping trying to run… and I'll soon be homeless come tomorrow at eleven o'clock when checkout time hits, and to top it all off I might have to call my stepdad who I hate to see if he'll Western Union me some help money." Sandra put her head down on the table and covered her face in shame. She started to cry softly.

Juliet felt sad for the girl. Her story sounded similar to hers not too long ago. She wanted to held her in some way. "Please don't cry," she told her, cautiously touching her shoulder. "What's your name?"

She composed herself and answered. "Sandra… Sandra McNeil." She sniffled, wiping her face. "I'm sorry for crying like this."

"It's all right. I was down and out like you not two weeks ago. Worse even. I'm talkin' almost ready to eat out of the trash down and out."

"Really? But you look so pretty," she complimented.

"Thank you," Juliet smiled, flattered.

"How'd you make it out? If you don't mind me asking."

"Well… I met a man, and he showed me the way. He showed me that I controlled the minds of men."

"Excuse me?" Sandra said, confused.

"I provide a service, an exclusive service," Juliet said.

Sandra thought for a moment, then it hit her. This beautiful girl was a prostitute.

"Oooh, you're a—"

"I'm a businesswoman. A liaison for the men in need of companionship of any kind," Juliet cut in and told her.

"Oh God... how old are you?" Sandra asked, curious.

"How old do I look?"

"Umm... twenty-two or twenty-three?" she guessed.

Juliet chuckled lightly. She liked the fact that outside of the bedroom people thought she was older.

"I'm seventeen," she told her.

"Seventeen?! Wow, we're the same age."

"Well, what do ya know," Juliet said sarcastically.

Just then, the register worker called over, alerting Juliet to her food being ready. She stood up and pulled a pen and piece of paper out of her purse. She wrote her number down and gave it to Sandra along with a twenty dollar bill.

"Here. Here's a twenty and my personal cell number. If you ever want to talk, just call me and I'll try and meet with you wherever, or, if you ever wanna become a businesswoman like myself and join a team like me... let me know. Take care, Sandra."

Juliet left and Sandra watched her. She sat looking at the twenty and the cell number a while after she was gone, then she ordered some food to go. She would take the long way around back to her motel. Tomorrow she would have to come up with a plan.

*   *   *

"And she looked like who? Justin Bieber's old girlfriend?"

"Mhmm, babe, she say she don't have any money to stay in her room—wherever that is—for no more days. I think she out here on her own like I was," Juliet told Romero. They were sitting on the bed back at the Lucky Nights Inn. The food from McDonalds lay between them as they ate and conversed.

"You gave her twenty dollars?"

"Uh huh, babe she needed it, plus I ran her a script just like you would have. When I left and looked back through the window, she was looking hard at my number... She gon' call, watch," she said, optimistic.

"She gon' call, huh?" Romero said, stuffing warm fries in his mouth. "And when and if she do, you gotta be smooth with me runnin' her down and givin' her these keys, plus you gon' have to school her to yo' techniques."

"Baby I know the deal, she gon' be second class, that's all."

"Sho' you right," he nodded while chewing. Romero looked at his watch and it was almost eleven o'clock at night. He wanted to get a few more pages typed out for his book so he got up and went over to the table and booted up his laptop.

Later on the next morning around three a.m. after Romero and Juliet had gone to bed, Juliet's phone chimed like a door bell. It rang several times before she rolled out of bed and answered it across the room. It could only be one person because the only people who had her personal cell were Romero and the girl she met at McDonalds. In the darkness of the room, she answered her glowing phone.

"Hello?" Juliet answered low.

"Oh, hey, it's Sandra, from McDonalds, um… I'm sorry it's so late, but I couldn't sleep."

"Don't worry about it. What's up?" Juliet asked. She looked about the room and everything was cloaked in shadows, the only light was the parking lot lights that made the closed curtains glow. Sandra continued.

"I'm sorry… I don't know why I called—"

"I do," Juliet cut in. "Sandra, it's okay… you want to know what I do in detail."

"How'd you know?"

"What do you wanna know?" Juliet said. She unplugged her phone from its charger and went into the bathroom.

"Well… do you like it?" Sandra asked. Juliet sat on the toilet lid.

"It's as good as you make it, and I choose to make it good most of the time. You see, Sandra, sex is just an action, a workout physically… but love, love is spiritual, a mental workout that strengthens a person to do the physical things that 'regular' people want."

"But how do I find love to give me that strength? It's not like I have time to look for a guy just to… you know."

"Sweetie, if you decide to join with me, I promise you you'll know love, maybe not as fast as me or in the same way, but if you're willing to learn and be schooled to this game… you'll be as happy as you want to be. Now, tell me exactly why you've called."

There was a pause on the line. Moments later, Sandra broke the silence and answered the question. "I called because I need money, and twenty dollars won't do."

"And you want to become a businesswoman such as me?"

"...Yes. Can you help me?" Sandra asked. She couldn't believe she had made the call, she couldn't believe she was even willing to come on board with such a profession, but she needed help and money and a place to sleep and a phone and everything above. Sandra had no choice, because going home wasn't an option.

"Where are you now?" Juliet asked.

"My motel, the Best Western down on Edison Avenue."

"Listen. Call a cab and tell them you want to go to the Lucky Nights Inn down on Fuller and Windlow, room 29. Pack all your stuff and bring it with you, all right?"

"Fuller and Windlow, room 29, yes, I'll be there," Sandra told her.

When the call ended, Juliet went back into the main area and over to the bed. She cut on t h e desk lamp and its bright light illuminated the darkness. Juliet sat next to a slumbering Romero and softly shook him awake. He squinted with a frowning face.

"Hmm, what?" he said, groggy.

"Baby," she called.

"Huh? Who?" he asked with closed eyes.

"The girl from the McDonalds, she called and told me she wants to be with us," she explained. One of Romero's eyes opened and looked up at her.

"Oh yeah?" he said.

Juliet nodded, smiling.

"And?" he asked, wondering.

"And she's on her way. I told her to call a cab over."

Romero sat upright and looked at the desk clock. "She on her way right now?" he asked, making sure he wasn't sleep-hearing.

"Right now," Juliet assured him. He blew out hot air with a head nod.

"Aight... let me get my mind right," he said, rubbing his face. He had strategy to go over in his mind.

Chapter 8

"Wow, you done been in some bogus shit since you been here," Romero said with surprise. He was sitting like a boss with his leg crossed, hand folded on his lap and Juliet standing behind him. The young beauty named Sandra stood before him telling him her story thus far. Romero was putting on the best boss impression he could because in reality he was just a regular nigga from Chicago who just so happen to luck up and find a willing female to be his "go-bot." Now he was faced with another potential moneymaker, except he would actually have to work to make her trust and love him... Just like Juliet. "So... here you are," he said, smiling. "You'd like to join the family I hear?"

"I'd like to make some money, yes," Sandra said awkwardly. She felt like a spelling bee student on stage. Who the hell were these people? she thought.

"You wanna make money then go beg on the corner for loose change... We make for the greater good of our team, our family, not for self. So... I'll ask again, and you need to be perfectly honest with yourself and me... Do you want to join the family?"

There was a long pause between them. Romero sat patiently. Sandra looked from his eyes to Juliet's who gave her no answer. She wanted money only, she wanted to do other things besides whore herself out, and she didn't know if "joining the team" meant she was locked out of pursuing her dream. She couldn't ask him just then so she took a chance.

"Yes... I want to be on your guys' team."

Romero clapped his hands together and smiled brightly. Juliet looked pleased as well.

"All right, welcome aboard. Juliet, bring her a chair so I can run her down," Romero said. Juliet took the other table chair and brought it over to Sandra. She sat down right across from him. From there, Romero gave Sandra the full rundown of the setup he and Juliet had going. He covered everything from prices to rules, from sexual acts, to the power she possessed and how to use it. Romero gave her the game just as he did Juliet only with extra on top, and Sandra seemed to take it all in without question. Romero schooled her until the dark sky turned blue without the sun. By the time he was almost done he was no longer sitting down but running elaborate skits and scenarios with Sandra. Juliet on the other hand had fallen asleep and was comfortably in the fetal position on the bed.

"And that's what it is," Romero finished. He sat down in his seat and took a swig of bottled water. "Now... before I close out all the way, 'm gonna shoot a bundle of questions out there to see if you was following. Ready?"

"Yeah, I'm ready," Sandra sighed. She was tired but completely engrossed by Romero's outlook on things and his easygoing nature. She liked him, and could see why Juliet loved him, he was very interesting.

"Aight... how much is yo' head game worth?" he asked.

"Forty to fifty bucks depending on how I feel," she told him.

"And the coochie game?"

"Sixty to a hundred, also depending on how I feel."

"Full package?"

"One-fifty, depending."

"What happen once a stud comes?" he asked.

"Umm... it's over, I get paid, but if he wants another round he has to pay to replay?"

"Right. Condoms?"

"Always, no latex on the dick... he can't stick?" she guessed.

"Right, right. What events happen after everything is said and done? What's M.C.S.?"

"Uh, um... Money, card, and shower," she remembered.

"Good. Any questions?" he asked, curious to hear what she might want to know.

Sandra thought for a moment. "A few, um... do I get to keep any of the money I make?"

"No," he said honestly. "I'm the king of the house. You will have access to money when you need something. If you want food, clothes, or simple miscellaneous things, I'll toss you what you need or go with you to get it, but as far as you yourself holding the money... no."

"Oh, okay—well, what about days off?" she asked.

"We work 24/7, 365. We just close and open at certain times. But once we reach a certain plateau in the game... things will change. I'm talking vacations around America and the world. Next question."

Sandra shook her head. She pretty much had everything stored in her mind. She was a call girl, and Romero was her pimp. Simple and plain. She had to see if it was going to work, because if it didn't… she would simply run away. "No more questions," she told him, yawning.

"Aight. I see you yawning, but we have one more piece of business to attend to before we rest, and that's putting you online," he told her.

"All right, what do I do?" she asked.

Romero got up and retrieved his computer and camera. He set everything up and started aiming the camera at Sandra.

"What's this?" she asked, puzzled.

"Just some random pictures for yo' Facebook page," he told her.

"I have a Facebook page already," she let him know.

"That's for Sandra McNeil, this… this is for clients, the thirsty trick-off artist who want to reach out and touch something. Stand up for me and pose with a smile."

Sandra did as he told her to and posed with a cheesy smile. He took several other pictures of her doing random acts. They were simple enough until she had to pose for her Craigslist picture.

"Take off your clothes," he told her bluntly. They were in the bathroom. Romero was standing in the doorway with camera ready.

"Huh?" Sandra asked, hearing what he said perfectly fine.

"Don't be shy around me, throw that shit away. Go 'head and take yo' sweater thing off and them jeans. I got to get a sexy picture for Craigslist," he said.

Sandra was nervous but did as instructed. When she stood in her bra, socks, and panties, Romero told her to sit on the sink and look sexy. As she did, Romero couldn't help but admire her perfect figure. Damn! he thought as he clicked away, she was so fucking bad. She was like a real model type. He could see the money rolling in for her, but he himself wanted to test ride her first, he just didn't know how to lay it on her yet.

"Aight, you good. Go on 'head and jump in bed with Juliet and get some rest, I got some shit to do on the computer," he told her. Sandra hopped down and began putting her clothes back on. As she did, Romero couldn't help but watch. He watched everything closely from her titties to her booty, and it turned him on. He had to go for it; he had to see where she stood with him being boss over her completely. So he took steps inside the bathroom and closed the door behind him. Sandra was pulling her shirt down but was still bottomless when she noticed he had come inside and closed the door.

"Who am I?" he asked, low and seductive. Sandra was caught off guard and a little bit unsettled as he stood in front of her. She didn't bother trying to put her pants on.

"You're Romero," she answered.

"And?"

"And... um... you're the king of the castle?" she guessed.

"Correct, and who are you?"

"The second queen."

"The second queen what?"

"The second queen-bitch?" she answered.

"Correct, and who bitch are you?"

"I'm yours... I guess," she said, seeming flustered.

"Sandra... do you guess or do you know?" he asked, taking a step closer.

She swallowed and cleared her throat. "I know... I'm your second queen-bitch," she told him.

"Good. So give your king a kiss," he told her.

Sandra hesitated for a moment but leaned over and kissed him light and quick.

"Baby girl... don't be shy, kiss your king like you mean it," he told her, licking his lip with low eyelids.

Sandra stepped up and gave him another kiss, only this time she added tongue and went deep. Romero took her by the waist and pulled her close. He slid his hands down to her butt and squeezed both her soft cheeks. It was nice and erotic, Sandra thought. She had never kissed or been with an African American before; there was a great shortage of black people in Maine. When they parted they were both stimulated, Romero's lower member was stiffening and Sandra's nipples were hardening. Looking deep into her hazel-green eyes, Romero unleashed his power of seduction upon her, a power males had over women in the heat of all moments.

"I want you to take off all yo' clothes, I'm about to bring you into this family through sexual marriage," he told her. Sandra did as he told her and shed all garments, and when she was in her birthday suit, he kissed her

66

lightly on the lips.

"Wait right here until I call you out, aight?" he told her.

"Mhmm," Sandra said, nodding.

Romero left and went over to Juliet who was still sleeping soundly. He came down upon her softly and kissed her lips and face until she woke. "Lil' mama, it's time for you to be tested, aight," he said.

"Mmm… all right, what is it?" she asked, squinting from the desk lamp.

"I need you to take them clothes off, get naked. I got baby girl naked in the bathroom. Me, you, and her finna become one… aight?"

Juliet was shocked and dumfounded; she didn't know what to think or say, but this was the game, this was the will of her man and she wouldn't turn him down now.

"All right, babe," she conceded. Both she and he got naked. Juliet got under the covers and Romero boldly went back to the bathroom to get Sandra.

"Baby girl, come on out," he called to her through the door. When she opened the door, Sandra was unprepared to see him naked, she could only guess that Juliet was naked as well and the three of them were about to engage in a threesome. Quickly Sandra scanned Romero's body and was pleased. He was nicely fit and the stereotype was true about black men… Romero was well hung.

Taking her by the hand, he led her out of the bathroom and into the main area. The two females looked upon each other with calm eyes. Romero came and sat on the bed, pulling her onto it with him. Juliet wasn't a lesbian, nor was Sandra, but in their minds, they were both bi-curious, and who better to try it with.

"Look," Romero began. "This is our world. We three are to become one unit right now. The shy, coy shit is out the window, ya'll two are about to become sisters. This right here is a circle of trust, a solid, unbreakable foundation. Aight?" he said, looking to them both. Both females gave confirmation. "Aight then… I want y'all to kiss, and do it like you kissin' me," he told them.

There was a pause at first. No one moved. Then, as the females looked and searched one another's eyes, Juliet came forward and Sandra met her halfway and they kissed. As their lips and tongues collided, Romero watched as his manhood rose to salute. He sat back and stroked himself until they parted.

"That was sexy as hell," he told them. "Baby girl, let's see how well you suck the dick." Sandra looked to Juliet for a second and then scooted over and began to suck Romero's dick. He bit his bottom lip as she slurped him down, then engaged in a hungry kiss with Juliet. Minutes into his oral session, Romero wanted to enter Sandra, so he stopped her and told her to get on her hands and knees. When he got behind her, he told Juliet, "Let her eat that pussy, lil' mama."

Neither Juliet nor Sandra protested, they just did as told. Now they were having a real threesome. Sandra began to lightly lick Juliet's pearl and Juliet's mouth hung open with wide open legs and frowned eyebrows. Romero slowly drove his cock into Sandra's tight, wet pussy hole and as he did, she couldn't help but moan softly. When he was all the way inside her, he gripped her hips and started to pump in and out of her.

"Ooh—ooooh, G-god, mmm, yesss," Sandra moaned with a rocking body. Romero and Juliet made eye contact. She smiled at him with a wide open mouth as Sandra dove back into licking and sucking on her entire vaginal area. The room was filled with sexual sounds: moaning and groaning, skin clapping together, squeaking bed rails. It was going down like never before and Romero was king. He had struck it rich with something more precious than gold, diamonds, or gems. He had pussy, the oldest money-making device in world history, continuous cash flow. This was the start of an empire. This was how he and his team would build their kingdom.

    *   *   *

Over that next month, the money came into Romero's pockets like "presto." Sandra was a sure thing for attracting creeps and when he profiles went live... she too was in high demand. Her first client was a guy from Florida. He was just passing through on business. His name was Carl Winters Jr. and he was part owner of a major fast food chain. Sandra made three hundred dollars that night and couldn't have been prouder. Romero got her a new cell phone and told her to continue holding onto her dream of becoming a model and actress. Client after client kept emailing and card after card was handed out to all the money holders. After three weeks the "Batphone"—as they called it—had over thirty clients logged inside. It sat on top of the TV like a homing beacon and when a client would call the ringtone would chime: "Pimp phone, pimp phone ringing." The girls were pulling in over $800 a day—sometimes more. Things were working so well, Romero rented the next room over which was equipped with a double bed. They used the single for business sessions only. Everything was running smoothly and there was never law trouble. The Lucky Nights Inn wasn't what you would call quality-rated, it was for lack of better words "ghetto," and ghetto folks minded their own business.

The bond between Romero, Juliet, and Sandra was strong. They were inseparable, and they did everything together and were content with the constant company of each other. Romero's mind frame had molded into this new 2013 version of a pimp. He dressed casual-urban but not flamboyant in colorful oversized suits. He treated his women like girlfriends and not street-corner property. He wasn't a "gorilla-pimp" like so many before him that demanded that his women make his money or he would beat her down, or even worse, kill her. No, Romero was caring and understanding, and that's what Juliet loved about him, and that's why Sandra was starting to. Everybody was happy in their position. The girls went shopping for what they wanted when they needed it, they bonded like best friends and shared sexual tips and stories from their past lives. Romero on the other hand sat back like a boss and collected money. Of course he too went shopping and was fresh in all the latest fashion but at the end of the day he craved cotton-printed dead presidents.

At the end of June, Romero was eighteen thousand dollars ahead and climbing. He never shared the total amount with the girls. Juliet wasn't even afforded that knowledge. Even though Romero had never had so much money before, it didn't change him nor did it overexcite him. The money simply drove him to become something bigger, to reach his goal of having a hundred thousand dollars or better. Romero had big dreams to get and live rich, and if he was going to accomplish that goal, he had to spend a little more cash on an eye-catching vehicle and look for a third queen to complete this trio. So, without telling the girls anything, he searched online for local vehicle deals and found the perfect machine. It was a used, all midnight blue 2005 Chrysler 300. It came completely standard and was owned by an older woman who passed away, leaving it to her son. The man asked for $9,500 but came down to a flat nine grand once Romero actually pulled out the cash in front of him. After the deal was struck, Romero took the car to the carwash and ran it through twice, then he paid twenty dollars to have it buffed-waxed by hand. When everything was done, the used car looked brand new. But that wasn't all Romero had been working on in secret while the girls had their backs turned. He had also been in online talks with local real estate agents and had taken interest in a nice three-bedroom apartment located close to Downtown Long Beach. The apartment's rent was pricy at eleven hundred a month but Romero made that in two days. He signed a year lease and paid first and last months' rent in cash. When he was done with all his business, he called Juliet on her cell phone.

"Hey, babe," she answered, knowing it was him.

"Come outside and see what I bought us," he told her. "And bring yo' sister."

Juliet instantly became excited and wide-eyed. Sandra sat on the opposite bed reading a tabloid magazine. She saw the look on Juliet's face.

"Girl what happened?" she said, sounding more urban.

"Girl, Romey said come outside and see what he bought."

Sandra's eyes widened. The girls scrambled to their feet and rushed to the door. When they came out onto the second floor platform, they looked down and saw Romero leaning against a new-looking car. They both were dumbstruck.

"Now I can't be having my girls walking and riding the bus forever," he called up, smiling. Both Juliet and Sandra came down and adored the vehicle with touchy approval.

"Rome, this is really, really nice," said Sandra.

"It is babe... How much did it cost?" Juliet asked.

"It ain't hurt nothing," he simply told her, unrevealing.

Juliet knew he never spoke about money numbers but she was just curious. She didn't care that he didn't tell her.

"Y'all go upstairs and gather up all our shit and bring it down," he told them, popping the automatic trunk.

"Why?" both Juliet and Sandra said in unison.

"Because... my queens deserve a castle, so I got them one." He smiled. Juliet and Sandra were cheerful and ran upstairs.

Chapter 9

Jennifer "Jennybell" Lente was tired, her feet were killing her and she was starving. She hadn't eaten a thing since breakfast and that was over twelve hours ago. Walking up and down the strip on Monroe Avenue was old and she was over it. It was overpopulated with seasoned streetwalkers who didn't take too kindly to new faces in their territory. Jennybell had been "hooking" for four months for a pimp named "West-Coast Red." He was black and rough on his girls. West-Coast Red was forty-eight years old and was still accustom to the old school way of pimping, which was overly charismatic, sleazy, and ill-tempered. Jennybell was a prime candidate for the line of work she was in, she knew. Sex always came easy to her and she liked it a lot. When she was only six years old, she used to rub her little "coo-coo" on the edge of the coffee table. When he was twelve, she let two boys her age touch all on her healthy developed body in the bathroom of their school. And when she turned fifteen she was caught riding her twenty-year-old boyfriend in her parents' bed. Jennybell was always a free spirit sexually and when she turned eighteen she packed her things, left Texas and headed for California. She had been there for two years.

Standing on a dark side street, Jennybell was dressed in a little black mini-dress that barely covered her large D-cup breasts and large ass. She stood 5'5" without heels but that night she was 5'11". She weighed 160 pounds and was considered thick by the black guys she knew and slept with back in Texas. Her skin was tanned, her lips full, and her brown hair was nicely styled. All in all, she looked cute. She wasn't fine or anything but she was extremely sexable. Jennybell waited with her arms crossed and saw a car parked down the street behind her. She could make out two figures inside and one seemed to be smoking because she could see the cherry on whatever it was glowing. When only the driver's head could be seen, Jennybell figured it was a hoe servicing a trick. Just then, as she was in thought with herself, an old school, candy-red Cadillac pulled to the curb with its lights off.

"Say hoe! How's it go?" West-Coast Red said. He was dressed from head to toe in Stacy Adams and puffed on a cigar. Jennybell said a shot prayer to herself as she bent down and looked through the passenger-side window.

"Red, it's dead out here tonight," she told him truthfully.

"Bitch! Don't make me get out this car, you been out here all day!" Now lay something on me before I place my foot up yo' fat ass!" he threatened.

Jennybell went inside her bra and hated to pull out what she had managed to make. She took it over and gave it to him. He counted it easily and was disappointed and angry.

"You funky bitch… this is forty dollars," he said, disgusted.

"West-Coast, it's slow, I told you that."

"You told me that? Bitch, don't move," he said, getting out.

Jennybell backed up, then she did her best to run.

*   *   *

The smooth sound of Usher's classic R&B album "Confession" played low through the interior speakers of the parked Chrysler 300. It had been a couple of weeks since the move from the Lucky Nights Inn and the Romero team was winning. Romero went from eighteen grand down to just under one thousand when he purchased the car and apartment. Once he and the girls went bargain shopping for furnishings, buying all the necessities such as beds, dressers, lamps, an entertainment center, and other miscellaneous items. When they were settled in, it was back to back business as usual because the Batphone waited for no one. Romero made a house rule. "Don't shit where you sleep," which meant never bring a client to the main palace. Romero kept the rooms open at the motel just for business use only. When the girls would book their clients, they would be driven over to the motel until the service was done. Romero would be in the double bedroom next door like always, just in case anything went south. The new setup was better because the girls had a place to really call "home," and at the end of the day, they all went home to a place unassociated with the work they did. Each person had their own room as well, even though they slept together in Romero's master bedroom, they still had the option to go into their own sanctuary and be alone. Romero's pockets were low after the furnishing process with not more than $3,200, but since the venue change, it seemed as if the girls put more effort into milking their clients and so he was well on his way back to stacking funds.

Now, as Juliet serviced Mr. Wonderful back at the motel, Romero and Sandra bent a block for a minute to smoke on a blunt of weed. Mr. Wonderful had become a repeat customer for her and he was the only client Romero trusted enough to leave her alone with for a while.

As Romero puffed on the strong intoxicating weed smoke, slouching low in his seat, Sandra bobbed her head and sang along to one of Usher's songs.

"What you know about this?" Romero asked Sandra.

"I know Usher," she told him, smiling in the dark.

"You know Usher, huh?" he said with smoke-filled lungs. He passed the blunt over to her and Sandra smoked. "Let me ask you a question, baby girl," he began. "Are you happy with me?"

Sandra blew out smoke and coughed lightly, shaking her head from the rush.

"Mhmm, yeah, I'm happy with you... why do you ask?"

"Just wondering," he shrugged. "Do you have love for me?"

Sandra smacked her lips, handing him back the weed. "Of course I do," she told him.

"Tell me," he said, putting the blunt to his lips.

"Romey... babe, you should know I love you," she said. And Sandra did, just as Juliet said she would. She had grown extremely fond of him and dependant on him. She felt she was his girlfriend, and number two was just that, a number, because when they made love or were alone, like they were then... it was he and her world.

"Tell me, I like to hear you say it from time to time," he told her.

Sandra was sitting on her knees and leaned over and came close to his ear. "I... love... you," she whispered. Sandra's warm breath tickled him and she kissed him there gently.

"Okay, okay, okay, hmm," Romero said, leaning up and unbuttoning his jeans. "You done started something now."

Sandra knew what he wanted and didn't mind at all giving him what he desired. She zipped his pants down, pulled his semi-hard dick out and gave it lip service. As she did, Romero continued to smoke. He was high as a kite as Sandra's warm mouth pleased his lower member. Then, up ahead outside, he noticed what could only be a streetwalker running from a man. The white girl had on high heels so she had no chance at evading her pursuer. In the dark of night, the man who wore a colorful pimp-suit sideswiped thee woman's feet and made her tumble to the fall-breaking grass. Romero simply watched, smoked, got head, and listened to music. The streetwalker raised a halting hand but only received a violent kick to her legs which jolted her entire body. Romero could hear no audio but he could guess that the verbal reprimand was harsh and threatening. When the black stud left and got back into the car, he drove past Romero. The girl was still sitting in the grass only twenty feet in front of him. She rubbed her tender leg. Romero started the car and slowly drove up next to the curb where the girl was.

"What are you—" Sandra began, but was shushed. she came up off him and wiped her mouth. She could see a girl sitting in the grass at the curb. Romero rolled down his window and leaned out.

"Rough night?" he asked sarcastically. Jennybell paused looking over at the man in the nice ride. She was in no mood for petty conversation unless it meant money.

"Can I help you with something? Are you looking to score, man?" she said, getting up.

"Yeah, you can help me with something… and yeah I'm lookin' to score. How much you chargin'?" Romero inquired, playing a role. Jennybell dusted her hands off, then her dress.

"Are you a cop?" she asked.

"Not at all, sweet thing."

"Well… what are you looking for?"

"What do you offer?" he asked.

"Twenty for a blowjob and forty for sex," she told him.

Romero whistled as if to say "wow."

"Who was the dude who treated you like shit a minute ago?" he asked, changing the subject. Jennybell frowned and was geared to walk off, but had to stick around just in case the guy wanted service.

"He was my brother. Look man, are you interested or not because I got work to do," she told him sternly.

"Slow down sweet thing, don't bite me. Look… how 'bout I give you forty dollars just for a half hour of yo' time? All I want is a conversation."

Jennybell was confused. What the hell was this guy on? she thought. But she needed the money. She couldn't go back to Red with nothing; he might kill her next time.

74

"What'll it be, sweet thing?" Romero asked, puffing the last bit of weed smoke and flicking the roach.

"Hey man, it's your money, and my name's Jennybell."

*   *   *

Back at the Lucky Nights Inn, Romero and Jennybell sat in the lot inside his car. He had sent Sandra up to the double bedroom so he could rundown Jennybell and see if she was interested in joining a winning team. Juliet was still next door with Mr. Wonderful, so Romero had just over thirty minutes to work his Chitown magic. Jennybell sat in the front passenger seat, there was no music on and the only light came from the parking lot lights and the midnight moon.

"My name is Romero, but my friends and people I like call me Rome," he told her, slightly turned in her direction.

"All right… Rome, what do you want to talk about?" Jennybell wondered.

"You… me… us… we. I want to know if you like suckin' dirty dicks in alleys and fuckin' unmonitored niggas in cars for peanuts? Are you okay with standin' on the streets all day and night making 120 to 200 dollars for a slick, slimy pimp? A pimp who verbally and physically beats you for some shit you may not always control?" Romero's words came at her steady and not insulting, and Jennybell was lost for words for a moment. She had asked herself those same questions time and time again. Who was this guy? she thought. Then, she answered.

"Why do you care? Are you a pimp or something?" she asked.

"Pimp is the title of a sleazy mufucka who only cares about two ultimate things… self and money. Me, I'm a king… and as a king, I have queens who serve their king honorably without threat, and without fear," he explained.

"Sounds like a pimp to me," she said honestly.

"Baby girl, right now one of two of my queens is servicing a client as we speak. At the end of the session she gon' be paid at least two hundred to three hundred dollars. She gon' shower afterwards and call her king—me—to take her home. You see, there ain't no forty or fifty dollars hits. There ain't so alleyways, back seats of cars or whatever… this is 2013, and times have changed. You out there at risk every day with the undercovers and the city cops. Granted we are at risk as well but it's ten times lower. My queens are always happy, they always good… can you say that? Yes or no?"

Jennybell hesitated with "no" in her mind but before she could answer, Romero cut back in. "Yo' hesitation means no. Baby girl, let's stick to yes and no answers, aight? Let's keep it real for the next twenty minutes, aight?" he asked.

"Aight… okay, let's," she said, getting ready mentally.

"Tell me… do you feel safe with yo' pimp?"

"Uh… not really," she said low.

"Do you love the nigga?"

"Hell no," she spat out, looking disgusted.

"Do you wish things would change for the better in your situation?"

"Yeah, every day," she admitted.

"Are you a street walkin' hoe? Or would you rather be a street ridin' pro?"

"Umm… a pro… I guess?" she shrugged.

"Baby girl, don't guess what you can be, know it. Now, would you like the opportunity to become a queen? To dress nice every day? To shop and get pampered at salons and massage parlors? To sleep in a comfortable bed of a palace on the tenth floor? To make thousands for yo' king each week servicing clients… clients, not alleyway tricks? Would you like to feel bonded to a team that moves as one unit, safe and sound? Tell me now… do you want to be on a winning team?"

Jennybell was engrossed in his words; it was like listening to the president give a speech during war. Hell yeah she wanted all he offered. Hell yeah she wanted to break free from West-Coast Red, but it wasn't that easy and she was scared to leave. "Man… you sound good and all but my so-called guy… my pimp, West-Coast Red… he won't stand for me just breaking bad on him," she told Romero seriously.

"Fuck dude, dude ain't shit but a washed-up-ass mummy! Do you want to be a queen and win?" he said sternly.

"Yeah, I do, but—"

"But nothing," he cut her off. "Do you wanna serve a king? Be a queen on a winning team?"

Jennybell sighed and conceded his offer. "Yes… I wanna be a queen."

"Good," Romero said, overjoyed inside his mind. "The old life you had is dead. All yo' old shit you had with dude is gone. You'll get all new stuff, fresh! This little talk was just the opening, I'm gon' school you till the sun come up, feel me?"

"Mhmm, I hear you," she said, nodding.

"Aight, come on, time to meet one of your sisters." Romero opened his door and began to get out. Jennybell followed. She was excited; it was as if a weight had been lifted off her shoulders.

*   *   *

Just like Juliet and Sandra before her, Jennybell was taken to school by Romero. When Juliet was done next door, she came over and was surprised to see the new girl, but once Romero filled her in on what was going on, she supported him 100% and took a seat across the room on the opposite bed from Sandra. Romero had his work cut out for him because this time he was dealing with a chick who already knew the game. Even though she hadn't been hoeing for too long, she still was well hip to the game and Romero had to de-brainwash her from the ways she thought she knew. So, for the first time, he allowed input from both Juliet and Sandra. Romero knew that if Jennybell heard the joy and compassion coming out of his women's mouths that his spiel would be ten times as powerful and enticing. So from midnight to midmorning, the three of them tag-teamed Jennybell with game and keys. Romero, as he would allow every so often, he allowed Sandra to take the car and go pick up breakfast from IHOP. Jennybell had respectfully told them that she was hungry and hadn't eaten in almost twenty-four hours. So when the food arrived, everybody took a slight break but the floor was still open with discussion. Jennybell was a smart girl and asked important questions. Most of her questions got answers she couldn't believe, which were the freedoms she would enjoy. Romero covered all grounds and made sure she understood that the old way was dead and the new way was alive. He and the girls dove into Jennybell's history and dissected it like a science frog. They asked her everything from her mother's name down to how many times she'd been in trouble with the law. They asked her sexual preferences, and everything in between, from swallowing come to anal play. What the three didn't expect was for Jennybell to be so open and so non-intimidated. She seemed open for anything on the sexual spectrum and eager to teach Juliet and Sandra who were still kind of novice some of her tricks. Romero could already see the dollars rolling in from Jennybell's services. He could see her being a specialist in all things taboo. She was just what he needed to complete his trio… a wild card.

When the dark a.m. sky turned from black to medium blue around five o'clock, Romero had just finished with the last part of his spiel. He had asked her the final questions just as he did Sandra and Jennybell answered them without stumbling. Normally everyone would have been tired but this time they were all still full of energy. Energy Romero had plans to burn off once he was finished setting up Jennybell's webpages, and when he was done he did just that.

"Aight, my queens, it's time to welcome your sister into the family the right way. Y'all start takin' them clothes off," Romero said as he shut down the computer. Juliet and Sandra started undressing with smiles on their faces; they were ready for the moment to come. But as they did, Jennybell was hesitant and Romero saw it in her body language.

"Baby girl, don't get nervous now," he said, kicking off his shoes. Juliet and Sandra looked at her, concerned, but kept undressing.

"It's not that, it's just… can I take a shower first because I like to be clean," she told them.

Romero stood up, pulled off his shirt, unbuttoned his pants and pushed them along with his boxer briefs to the ground. He stood stark naked and caught Jennybell's wandering eyes on his dick. Romero, without fear, casually came over to her and took her by the hand.

"'mma take one with you." He looked at Juliet and Sandra and winked. "Y'all go 'head and get started." He led Jennybell into the bathroom while Juliet and Sandra happily got in bed with each other.

Chapter 10

Even though Jennybell wasn't as attractive as Juliet and Sandra she still did numbers. Once her profiles went live and the creeps peeped her fresh face... they came slow but surely. Romero was a good dude but he was no fool, he kept an eye on her once he moved her in and told his other two women to do the same. Jennybell was already well trained to be obedient and so she had no problem being told she wouldn't receive her own cell phone until Romero felt she was fully disconnected from contacting her old pimp. But Romero did take her on a small shopping spree, spending over three grand on her new wardrobe, and also taking her to the hair salon and nail shop. Jennybell's first client was a construction worker from the Bay Area, his name was Collen Berner and he was said to be in town on a three-day job building a three-car garage for a movie starlet. Jennybell worked him over for two hours. She gave him anal sex and made him come more than three times. By the end of the session, Collen had paid her his entire check for forty-eight hours of work and was highly satisfied. When he received his call card, he promised he would use it soon, and when Romero came into the room once the client left, he found Jennybell in the shower and seven hundred and fifty dollars on the nightstand. And that's how it was with almost all of her clients. They would want to be with her every so often but when they did call... she put the sex down very well.

And so the house of Romero was built. The four of them forged a solid bond dipped in trust, respect, and love. Money was being made at a steady pace and the clients kept coming. By the end of the last of June the Batphone had well over double the numbers it held the last time. It held the numbers of teachers, college students, doctors, storeowners, and a number of other professions. Things seemed perfect. Everything was as it should have been and everyone was content, if not happy. Romero felt like the luckiest man in the world. He had made over twenty-five thousand dollars and the savings were climbing every day. He owed it all to one person in the long run, Juliet, his ace, his number-one queen. Her light continued to shine as brightly as the day they first crossed paths. She kept the peace between the queens and led when Romero needed her to. She was his key... and he was secretly in love with her.

"Chop, chop, ladies!" Romero said as he impatiently waited in the kitchen area. "These are reservations."

"Here we come, babe," Juliet yelled from the back area. All three of the women were finishing up getting dressed. Romero was taking them out as a surprise celebration for them working so hard over the last month. He was taking them not too far from the apartment to a five-star restaurant called Emerald's. He had made the reservations over a week prior because secretly he was about to reach his halfway mark of fifty thousand dollars. So the dinner was to celebrate that as well, only the girls didn't know that part. Romero was dressed in a form-fitting three-piece suit by Luigi Bianchi Mantora, which was paired with Johnston and Murphy shoes and a Swarovski-Piazza Grande Quartz watch. He was looking like a boss and felt like one because he had never spent four grand for a single outfit. Minutes later the girls each emerged one by one from the back. Jennybell came out first. She was dressed in an elegant Donna Karen dress. Sandra was second in a sexy fitting pencil skirt by Vera Wang, and lastly Juliet came out in a tight-fitting miniskirt by Chanel.

"Mm-mm-mm, y'all look good enough to eat! Y'all look like movie stars on a red carpet," Romero stood and complimented. Each female was smiling and posing for him. They cherished compliments from him.

"You look good too, Romey," Sandra was the first to say.

"Mhmm, like a CEO," added Jennybell.

"Like a true king, babe," Juliet finished.

Romero knocked invisible dust off his shoulder and fixed his jacket. He blushed a little.

"Thank you, thank you, now let's ride out before we late," he told them. They all headed downstairs. It was July 1st, 2013, on a warm Friday night when Romero and his ladies pulled up to Emerald's. The valet took the key to the Chrysler and parked it while the party of four entered the restaurant. Once inside, they were seated in a comfortable corner booth with a view of downtown. The place was packed with people who all dressed as if they were multimillionaires. There was even a few cast members from the blockbuster hit movie Twilight: Breaking Dawn. Soft classical music played softly overhead as patrons dined and conversed in low tones.

"Good evening, my name is Crystal and I'll be your service this evening. Would you like a wine menu first?" the bubbly waitress asked. Coming over, Romero looked around the table but got no help with making a decision so he handled it his way.

"What's the price on your cheapest red wine?" he asked without shame.

The waitress thought for a moment. "It's Pneu, early year, 2003. It's $100 a bottle," she informed him. Romero saw from the corner of his eyes the girls look to him but he played his role, and without pause he told the waitress, "All right, we'll have a bottle."

"Excellent choice. Would you like menus?" she asked him.

"No ma'am, we'll each have the porterhouse steak, medium well-done. Also, two fresh garden salads with French dressing and ranch dressing on the side." Romero had to take command.

"Excellent. Your order will be about ten minutes but in the meantime, I'll return with your wine selection," the waitress said, smiling as she turned and left.

"So… all y'all good with what I ordered?" he asked, unbuttoning his jacket and placing an arm on the back of Juliet's chair. All three told him yes. Moments later, the waitress returned with the wine which was on a wine tray sitting in ice. She popped its cork and poured each person a half-glass before she left again.

"A toast," Romero said, lifting hiss glass to the center of the table, "to my three favorite women in the world."

All four glasses met and clanked with a toast and they sipped.

"So… y'all ready to fly to Chicago for the fourth?" he asked them.

"Oh, I can't wait to see the city," said Sandra.

"I'm ready," said Jennybell.

"I can't wait to see yo' mama and see what you gon' say when she ask who we are," Juliet said, smiling.

"My mama cool, she don't care about what or how I do, as long as 'm not in jail and alive she good. All y'all my women… she don't need to know no more than that," he told them, sipping more wine. Romero's mother and family threw a Fourth of July barbecue every year in Garfield Park. It was a family affair each time but every year damn near the whole neighborhood would come out and kick it. Romero had never missed an event and his mother begged him to come home. She was hearing good things from him when he would call her, plus he would send her cash in the mail sent through overnight express.

Ten minutes after the wine came, their food arrived hot and smelling delicious. They all joined hands to bless the meal, and when they were done, they ate and enjoyed their time together. About thirty minutes later each person had eaten what they could, but saved room for dessert. Romero ordered a classic slice of cheesecake with strawberry ganache. All three women ate their slice with sweet delight. The night was going well without a hitch; the girls were telling Romero a funny story about a show they watched on television called Toss.0. When they had told him the climactic ending, they all laughed in jollity. but then a person's presence and voice cut in.

"Well, I'll be a rat's ass on Sunday morning. Hey hoe, where you been hidin'?"

Everyone's face at the table was wiped clean of their smiles, Jennybell's especially. Standing right next to her was her old pimp, West-Coast Red, Romero figured as much. he was dressed in a deep purple suit with black pen-stripes. His mouth had teeth capped with gold and all his fingers had gold rings. He reminded Romero of the late, great, Benny Mack, and to his right side stood a fine chocolate sister whose dress matched his suit. No one at the table spoke. It was awkward, and Juliet and Sandra were confused looking back and forth from everyone. West-Coast Red spoke down at Jennybell but seemed to address Romero.

"Say, youngsta… so you the one who stole my golden goose, huh? Got her all dolled up and everything. Say hoe, greet a pimp when you see me," Red said. Jennybell cleared her throat and her head started to lift as if to comply, but Romero cut in.

"Say man, can't you see we tryna build right here? You got the wrong table, ain't no hoes over here."

But Red didn't even look Romero's way; he just continued to look down upon Jennybell who looked like a frightened child. "Did you think you could hide in plain sight? Huh hoe? Bitch, I own you," he said low and snakish. Jennybell lashed out about to tell him he didn't own her but as soon as she did, West-Coast Red smack-grabbed the back of her head. Jennybell shrieked saying "ah," and Romero quickly started to rise up but was halted by the flash of a gun tucked into Red's front waistband. Romero froze in anger and slowly sat back down. The people in the restaurant were oblivious to what was going on because of the area they were in. Juliet and Sandra were caught off guard and were frightened as well. They looked on at the scene with sadness for their sister.

"Bitch, I'll kill yo' funky tramp-ass here and now," West-Coast Red said, yanking Jennybell around. He then turned and looked at Romero. "What you godda say, nigga?"

Juliet and Sandra looked to him as well. Romero was filled with rage. He wasn't scared of the man, just his gun.

"What the hell you want, man?" Romero asked calmly.

"The cash this hoe was gonna make me from her ass," he told him. Jennybell's head was cocked to the side and her face was twisted in pain.

"How much is that?" Romero asked, cool-headed with locked eyes.

"Let's see… it's July, she been gone since June… six months… 120 a night times thirty… hmm, the bitch owe me at least twenty thousand," he guesstimated.

"Twenty? Done, can you give me a few weeks?" Romero asked.

"You gotcha two weeks, youngsta," he said, releasing his grip on her hair. He also covered his gun back up. "She know where I be… two weeks, and if you skip town, you better neva come back cause you do… it's a murder scene."

"You gon' get what you got comin', homie, don't trip. Two weeks… and when you paid, your hands are off," Romero told him.

"Mhmm," Red said, adjusting his suit jacket while backing up. "Y'all folks enjoy ya cheesecake."

Then he was gone. Juliet and Sandra rushed to Jennybell's side, cooing and giving her comfort. She had tears in her eyes and told them that she was all right. Romero was livid. He was sitting wide eyed with clenched teeth, flexing his jaw muscles. His heart was racing and he wished he was back at home with his guys. They would have hunted West-Coast Red down that very night and killed him and his hoe. Romero didn't even notice that he had a hand clenched full of the table's covering until Juliet called to him, snapping him out of his zone. When Romero focused, he looked into the eyes of three females who looked concerned for him.

"I'm sorry, Rome," Jennybell apologized. He swallowed and calmed himself down.

"No need to be sorry," whatchu sorry for?" he asked sternly. Jennybell shrugged, looking sad.

"What you gon' do, babe?" Juliet asked, concerned.

"We gon' go to Chicago… eat some ribs, burgers… we finna celebrate the Fourth," he told them.

"But what about that guy? And what he said?" asked Sandra.

"Let me worry about him… I'll take care of dude."

*   *   *

Once the plane landed at O'Hare Airport, Romero and the girls took a cab down the Eaton's Expressway to the Westside of Chicago. It felt good to be back in familiar territory as Romero played tour guide for the girls who had never been and were marveling at the city's skyline. Twenty-five minutes later when the cab made it out west to Romero's area called Capitol Hill they pulled into his mother's driveway of her brownstone row house. Romero could tell by the cars parked out front and a couple of his little cousins running around that the family had already started to gather. As Romero paid the toll fare, he and the girls filed out with their single bags. The hot Chicago heat was in full effect but the day was bright and cloudless. Making their way up and into the house after greeting a couple of his aunts and uncles, Romero guided his women through his childhood home and found his mother in the kitchen. She was sitting at the dinner table with her back to him. She smoked on a Newport cigarette and gave his uncle-in-law, Dave, directions as to how to load the meat-cooler correctly. Romero caught Dave's eyes and gave him the "shush" finger just before he came up behind her and playfully whispered into her left ear.

"That ain't how you pack no cooler," he teased in a deep voice. Mrs. Hinton, better known to the neighborhood as Mama Ree, flinched to one side with a start. Then once she saw that it was her only son, she smiled happily and embraced him around the neck.

"What up, Dave?" Romero said, presenting a fist.

"How ya been, nephew?" Dave asked, fist-bumping him.

"Maintaining," Romero responded. Mama Ree turned in her seat and was surprised to see the three white girls standing in her doorway.

"Who are these girls?" she asked, looking puzzled.

"These my lady friends," he began. "This is Juliet, Sandra, and Jennybell. Ladies, this is my mother. Call her Mama Ree."

"Hi, Mama Ree," all three said in unison.

"Oh Lord, what has my son been up to?" she said, looking the girls up and down. All three girls smiled at her warmly, but inside they were all slightly nervous.

"Son, you look good. Did you just get in?" she asked.

"Thank you. Yeah, we just got out the cab. Where everybody else at? Down at the park?" Romero asked, leaning against the sink.

"Mhmm, yo' cousin and the rest of them down there. They should have everything set up, the first load of meat and food done been cooked and stuff. We all just came to get the rest of the stuff," she explained to him.

"Oh, okay, aight, let's get movin' cause we hungry, ain't we ladies?" All three girls nodded in agreement. "What you need us to do? What do you need carried?" Romero asked, rubbing his hands together.

"Them cases of pops and that other cooler with the liquor in it," Mama Ree told him.

"Okay, ladies," he said, looking over to the trio. "Grab them cases of pops and go with my unc' to his truck."

One by one, the girls did as they were told and followed Romero's uncle out the back door to his truck in the driveway.

"Rome," his mother called, smacking him lightly on his thigh. "Boy... who is them white girls?"

He frowned and smiled with a look that said "What?"

"Mama... I told you they my friends," he said, lying badly.

"Boy... you better be careful with whatever you got goin'."

"Got goin' what? Man I'm ready to eat, that's what's goin' on," he said, rubbing his stomach.

"Mhmm, okay... anyways, you got some money for me?"

"How much? For what?"

"For some smoke. Them boys on Aston got some kush."

"How much you need?" he asked, digging in his pocket.

"Enough for two quarters, so... about eighty, ninety bucks."

"Damn," he said, peeling her off a one hundred dollar bill. "You need to stick with regular grade cause that's crazy." From there, Romero and his family headed over to Garfield Park. When they got there, they could see everyone gathered around in a designated area. There were about thirty people in all, and balloons and colorful streamers were nicely placed on the park picnic tables.

Three or four of Romero's little cousins ran up to them happily as they all exited their vehicles. When they made their way over to the barbecue area, everyone who knew Romero well greeted him with open arms. Juliet made sure she was close on his arm to solidify her high-ranking position. The three queens were like white dots on a black board, they were the only whites in attendance. But Romero made sure he introduced them as his "lady friends" to all he greeted and greeted him.

The music played loud through the speakers of the iPod and dock with crystal-clear clarity. The rap artist 2 Chainz rhymed steady to his street classic mix CD called "Tru Religion." Children were at play while grown folks conversed in circles and groups. By midday, the number of people at the barbecue had doubled like every year. It almost made an unknown passerby think they were seeing a family reunion. Sitting at one of the picnic tables set asides just for dining, Romero and his white queens feasted on finger-licking food. A few of Romero's female cousins had found their way over and opened up a dialogue with the three girls about life outside Chicago and of course the fashionable clothes the three had on their backs. Romero was pleased to see that the awkward stage—as far as the three girls being white and "lady friends" of his—was basically over. Some of his family members even addressed the girls by name. Romero put on a smile but was at times deep in thought about his dilemma back in Cali. He was raised to deal with aggression and deathly threats only one way… mirrored force.

"What up, bitch-ass nigga?" a voice called to Romero from behind. He instantly smiled with knowing and twisted around.

"What up, bitch?" Romero said playfully. He greeted his younger cousin with a loving handshake and hug.

"Willie can't be over here, he barred," one of their female cousins blurted out. Romero shook his head.

"Shut the hell up, nosy," Willie snapped at the girl. She rolled her eyes waving him off. Willie "Nuk" Hinton was an only child like Romero. In fact, there were four elder sisters, Mama Ree, Auntie Gwyn, Auntie Pearl, and Auntie Missy. All four sisters had only one child each, and Willie and Romero were the oldest and closest. Nuk was nineteen years old, 5'8", 175 pounds, black and night, and had short six-inch dreadlocks. Nuk was a gangbanging public menace. He was raised in the system, the juvenile detention center used to keep a bed open for him. People were cautious around when he came around, and rightfully so because Nuk had a wild temper and was known to fly off the handle at a drop of a hat. He was nineteen and had already shot at and maybe even killed more than five people. Thing was, Nuk never scared Romero. He was the only person Nuk trusted wholeheartedly.

After introducing the girls to his cousin, Romero pulled Nuk to the side to have a private conversation. They walked to the parking lot and leaned against random family cars.

"Cuz, dem all yo' hoes?" he asked, wide eyed.

"Ain't no question," Romero admitted.

"Daaamn… look at cuz, you doin' it like dat, bro?"

"Doin' it like that," he boasted, giving him dap.

"Let a nigga slide in a fuck somethin'," Nuk asked bluntly.

"Which one?"

"Anyone. The thick one."

"Oh, you talkin' 'bout Jennybell," Romero told him.

"Yeah, shordy d-so," Nuk nodded with a devilish grin.

"'mma think on it and see what's up, but first let me holla atchu on some street shit first."

"What? Mufuckas out there in Cali on bullshit? You need me to come out there and show a nigga how Chitown get down?"

"Yeah, it's somethin' like that. Some weak-ass old-school pimp-ass nigga basically upped pistol on me."

"Oh yeeeah?"

"Yeah. the nigga threaten to 'change' a mufucka and everything. Tryna extort me for twenty bands and all dat.

"Nuk's eyes opened wide. He crossed his arms about his chest and was interested even more. "Twenty bands? Nigga, he think you holdin' twenty rocks?"

"Nuk, cuz… twenty rocks ain't shit to me, I make that a month. What 'm sayin' is I ain't payin' shit! And I ain't finna be duckin' no nigga."

"So what's up? You wanna 'body' dis nigga or what?" Nuk asked.

Romero paused for a moment. "Gots to, cuz… got to. But peep

game, 'mma need you to drive out there cause I ain't got no burnas out there, yo' car still run d-so?" Romero asked.

"Hell yeah, but I ain't drivin' all the way to Cali, nigga."

"Cuz... aight—look... I'll give you ten rocks," Romero said.

"Ten bands?!" Nuk repeated.

"Ten bands. Five now and five once you get to the crib."

Nuk thought to himself. He wanted the money bad as hell, but he hated to drive long distances with weapons in his car. He loved his cousin though, and he couldn't deny him in a time of critical need... plus he really wanted that money. "Aight, fuck it, I gotchu, cuz," Nuk decided. "But I need the five now and a shot of ol' girl pussy."

Romero pulled out his billfold and counted off five thousand dollars and handed it to him, then he rolled over to Jennybell and waved her over. "Where your car at?" Romero asked Nuk before she made it over.

"On the other side," he told him.

Finally Jennybell made it over. Romero hugged her waist and kissed her lips. "Baby girl, I need you to handle something for me, it's very important," he said to her. Jennybell frowned and looked from him to Nuk.

"Whatchu need, Rome?" she asked.

"'mma need you to lay it on my cousin here, no charge. He gon' be drivin' out to Cali later on tonight and he gon' meet me there in a couple of days... we got some West-Coast Red business to handle." Jennybell understood what he meant and was in awe about it, but she played it cool. She looked to Nuk and nodded. "Good girl," Romero said, planting another quick kiss to her lips. "Go on 'head." Jennybell followed behind Nuk and they went to his car on the other end of the park.

Romero stood in the lot for a moment thinking to himself. He looked out into the sea of people and caught Juliet's eyes on him. He nodded his chin up at her and smiled, then she did the same.

Chapter 11

It was half-past one in the morning back in Long Beach when Romero got the call from his cousin that he had entered the city limits. He and the girls had enjoyed three days in the Midwest and had flown back the night before. Ever since he had returned, he couldn't stop contemplating the task he had to handle. He thought he had left his cowboy days back on the cold streets of Chicago… but he guessed that when you're on top, someone always tries to pull you down.

Once his cousin called back and informed him that he was not too far away, Romero woke and gathered the girls in the living room. All three of them sat on the couch knowing something was wrong. Juliet slept with him every night and she saw his inner torment.

"Babe, what's this all about? It's late," Juliet asked as she wiped sleep from the corner of her eye. Romero stood before them fully dressed with his hands crossed in front of him.

"My cousin Willie is on his way here, y'all may remember him from the barbecue. Anyways, he and me got some business to handle so 'mma need y'all three to chill out here until I contact y'all. If… if I call collect from jail, don't trip, I don't plan on going to jail but if it happens just come bond me out if possible… and I'll tell y'all the combo to the safe. That's all."

The girls were confused and didn't understand, the looks on each of their faces said as much. "Jail?" Juliet spoke up. "Babe… whoa… can you tell us what's going on?"

"Better if you don't know, Jay. Just know that you'll be in charge if shit go south," he told her.

"Rome, this wouldn't have to do with that pimp guy would it?" Sandra asked.

"Yeah, please don't get yourself caught up, Rome, we need you out here," added Jennybell. Romero felt bad for them and he felt their love at the same time. He came over, stepped around the coffee table and sat in front of them. He held out his hands and all three placed one of their hands in his. He spoke gentle and calm.

"Aight, look… this kingdom we have don't bend to threats. Your king… your man does not fold for no man who bleeds red like him. Now, y'all all my queens and I got more love for y'all than anyone… so don't trip. Everything's gon' be good. No more questions, just obey me on this and remember what I said… aight?" Romero looked at each girl and each one nodded with compliance. "Aight, gimme kiss," he said to Jennybell first. He kissed them all. Seconds later the apartment wall-speaker buzzed, indicate that someone was downstairs.

"That's him now," Romero said standing up and retrieving a duffel bag left next to the kitchen counter. All three girls stood up and slowly followed him to the door. Juliet led the way.

"Babe," Juliet called as he opened the door. "Please be careful and come back home."

He winked at her and left.

* * *

When Romero and Nuk got into the black 2002 Land Rover, he was directed to the Lucky Nights Inn. Once they entered the double-bedded room, they dispensed with the formality and got down to business.

"What you bring?" Romero asked him. They both were getting dressed in all black clothes that Romero provided.

"A 9 and a sawdy," Nuk told him. Romero already knew that he would handle the 9 millimeter and Nuk would have the sawed-off shotgun. The cock read 2:15 a.m.

"'mma hold down the 9," he told Nuk.

"Aight, bet," he agreed.

"We gon' stake dis nigga spot out and try to hit his ass whenever he come outside, dark out or light out," Romero told him.

"Aight, you know 'm up with all bullshit, just tell me when to go," Nuk said easily. "You know where the bitch lay at?"

"My number three gave me the 'vic's' address, phone number, and everything. You ready?" Romero asked.

"Born ready, nigga," Nuk said.

West-Coast Red lived out in the better part of Long Beach, the middle-class area that catered to all nationalities. His house was the second house in from the main avenue that ran through most of the city. When Nuk's black SUV turned onto Red's street they saw his Caddy parked in the driveway. There were lights on throughout the house. There was a small park that separated the neighborhood in the middle and Romero told Nuk to park across the street from Red's house. The small residential neighborhood was dark and quiet; the only light came from the main avenue and select lamp posts that glowed softly like decorations. With reclined seats Romero and Nuk stalked in the truck's cockpit.

"So what... we wait?" Nuk asked with a whisper.

"Hell nah, I was at first but 'mma call the nigga and tell him to meet me so he can get the money. When he come out then we dump on his ass," Romero said with equal low tones. He then pulled out his phone and called. It rang twice before it was answered.

"Who call me unknown?" the male voice asked, sounding irritated.

"This youngsta, I got yo' chop," said Romero.

"Dig dat... I knew you was smart. Where you at?"

"At the carwash down on Coop."

"The Soap Dish?" he asked.

"Yeah. When can you get here?"

"Gimme ten minutes," Red told him.

"Aight, ten minutes," Romero repeated before hanging up. "Let's ride, cuz," Romero said, pulling out his gun and cocking it. Both he and Nuk exited the truck and jogged across the street as quiet and as stealthily as an alley cat. Up the lawn they went until they were posted in the shadows undetected on the side of his house. Both men's adrenaline rushed through their veins as they waited with focused minds and racing hearts. West-Coast Red had a large porch that extended almost the entire face of his house. There was a crawl space but it was fenced. Romero figured he would just have to select a kill option once he came outside. Voices came from inside the house but were inaudible. Then, seconds later, the front door came open and someone came out. Romero carefully peeked around the corner and saw West-Coast Red standing on the porch, putting on his suit jacket. In the door behind him was a woman who had to be one of his hoes because Romero heard "Daddy" come out her mouth. There was no more time to waste, so Romero sprang into action and rounded the corner with haste, but as he did and raised his gun to fire, he tripped over a lawn sprinkler and stumbled to the ground with a light thud. West-Coast Red saw him and was startled.

"What the fuck?!" he flinched instinctively, reaching for his gun in his waistband. But Nuk had already taken aim on the side of the porch and squeezed off a shot. The sawed-off shotgun exploded like a cannon and sparks lit up the darkness like a camera flash. The buckshot splintered the screen door and the pellets from the shell tore into West-Coast Red's left shoulder, sending him ducking for cover. The woman in the doorway screamed and slammed the door. Romero scrambled back onto his feet and sent his own shots at the man. Romero's aim was off by a mile and Nuk's second attempt was off as well. West-Coast Red crashed through his porch's wooden guardrail and fell to the driveway below. There was a row of hedges that divided the property line of the house next door. West-Coast Red sprinted and dove through them for dear life as Romero gave chase with rapid fire. When Romero came out the other side, he collided with a parked car and immediately ducked for cover as return shots were fired in his direction. West-Coast Red was shooting blindly as he fled into the neighbor's backyard. Nuk emerged through the hedges beside his cousin and wasted no time locating Red and taking off after him. Romero followed behind him and the two of them were now in a foot race with Red. Surprisingly agile, Red jumped the fence and continued running down the alley. He left off two more blind shots at his pursuers but missed.

Romero and Nuk leaped the fence with ease and paid no attention to the shots fired at them. They took off running after Red and gained on him quickly. "Buss, cuz!" Nuk commanded. Romero raised his gun and let off three shots. West-Coast Red cried out in pain as he was hit in the back. He crashed wildly to the rocky gravel below.

"Ahhh... Lord help me mama!" shouted Red in agony. But Romero and Nuk did not hesitate to end his life as soon as they made it upon him. The echo of their final shots vibrated the neighborhood like rolling thunder. Agitated dogs throughout the area barked hysterically.

"Come on, cuz." Nuk tapped Romero on the chest. They hopped another fence and crept low and quickly until they emerged back in the front of the neighborhood. When they peeped out from around the random house, they were three houses down from where the truck was parked. Many lights were now on inside most of the neighboring homes and they were sure that the police were on the way.

"Fuck," Romero whispered. "Come on," Romero said, sprinting as fast as he could down to the truck. Nuk followed close behind. Once they made it back, they started the engine and drove off without the aid of headlights. "Drive slowly, Nuk… and head for the highway," Romero told him.

They drove smoothly under the cover of darkness through the rest of the neighborhood until they came to the main street on the other side. Once it was safe, they hit their headlights and headed for the nearest highway.

 * *   *

It was almost four in the morning and Juliet along with the other girls sat around the front area of their apartment, each one deeply worried about Romero's safety since he had not returned nor contacted them yet. All three women held onto their cell phones in anticipation that he may contact them first. Jennybell sat on the kitchen barstool, Sandra on the couch, and Juliet stood by the window. None of them spoke, they only waited. Suddenly Juliet's cell lit up and chimed the song "Big Pimpin'" by Jay-Z. She answered it and the other girls looked over to her.

"Hey, babe, what… uh-huh… all right… okay, we're on our way right now. Bye." Juliet hung up and smiled.

"What he say?" Sandra asked, standing.

"He's good, he said to come pick him up about half a mile out of town at a rest stop and diner called Mack's and bring him a change of clothes."

Both Sandra and Jennybell sighed with relief.

"Come on, let's not keep him waiting," Juliet said.

 * *   *

When Romero and Nuk got to the rest stop, they immediately parted ways. Nuk was given his money, and after brief words of care, hit the highway back to the Midwest. An hour later after Romero made the call home, his three queens pulled up outside the building and he left and go t in. After changing into another outfit and tossing the other in the trash they headed back home.

Later on that day, the news broke with its top story and it was the shooting death of forty-nine-year-old Pervis Jackson. Romero and the girls sat around the living room watching while eating a family meal from KFC. Once the news reporter stated that the police have no solid eyewitnesses or suspects, Romero turned the channel to another program. None of the girls spoke about what they saw or what they thought, they just gave one another knowing glances and returned to eating.

From there it was back to business. The Batphone had been cut off for five days and once it went back live, it was packed with messages, and the main email address was packed as well with new and old faces. The money that Romero invested with his cousin was made back within days, and just like always the numbers flipped and flipped.

By the end of September, Romero's kingdom was worth well over one hundred grand but there were no signs of stopping. Romero spoiled his queens, buying them anything they desired badly. If it was $700 heels, they got them. If it was a $1,500 dress, he bought it. If they wanted lobster, crab, shrimp, or steaks for dinner, they ate it. Money became no object because the girls became masters of their bodies and their sexual talents. After a while, Romero made the decision to remove any and all profiles linked to the girls and simply cater to the hundred clients that were logged into the Batphone. Romero wasn't naïve in thinking that his operation couldn't be destroyed by the federal authorities so he wanted to limit the business he did to a more private avenue. He wanted to protect himself as well as his girls so he also opened up a bank account in Sandra's name and placed his money in a safety deposit box with a contractual agreement that only allowed him access to its contents.

By December, Romero wanted to celebrate the holiday and the New Year in style, so he surprised the girls with a trip to New York City. Juliet was especially happy because it was one of her dream destinations. They flew out on a Monday afternoon and arrived Tuesday morning at JFK International Airport. It was a sight to see and a wonderful winter wonderland decorated with Christmas lights, wreaths, and other seasonal figures. Romero checked himself and the girls into the Hampshire Hotel which was almost in the heart of the city. It stood not one block away from the Rockefeller Center and the world-famous Radio City Music Hall. They reserved a presidential suite on the top floor with a city-wide view. The girls were in awe and were overjoyed like children on a field trip. They toured the city, going to The Museum of Modern Art, Whitney Museum of American Art, Times Square, Central Park, and shopping at the Manhattan Mall. New York was a magical place during the Christmas holiday, and on Christmas morning, the girls woke Romero up with gifts. Romero was thankful for his presents and almost shed a tear, but it was the women who cried when he presented each of them with diamond-encrusted platinum rings from Tiffany's. He got down on one knee and took all three of their hands and professed his love and honor for them all. He told them to not be afraid of worldviews of relationships and know that love can be shared equally with people who hold it secret. And once the countdown commented from ten to one, bringing in the New Year days later, Romero and his queens stood on the top floor of their hotel and watched the ball drop. After toasting to "family and new beginnings," Romero and his queens christened the New Year with a bed-filled sexual romp.

*　*　　*

"Hello, Mr. Marlongo, so nice of you to call, this is Sweet Thing. How can we service you?" Jennybell said after answering the Batphone. That was how all the girls answered the phone. They would read the name on the caller ID, state their nickname—which was Sweet Thing for Jennybell, Sweet Baby for Juliet, and Baby Girl for Sandra—then ask what service they wanted. Each queen had "subjects" or clients that called only for them, and Mr. Marlongo was a paralegal at a law firm who usually called for Sandra.

"Hey, I'm calling because I went online and none of you girls are posted anymore," he said.

"Yes, well, we are dealing only with exclusive clients now and will not be adding to the client list anymore," she explained to him. They had been getting a lot of calls concerning their online profiles and all three girls were used to answering the inquiries.

"Oh… well that's too bad, because I have a friend who is very interested in becoming a client. He's very rich, and I recommend him highly," Mr. Marlongo told her.

"And what does he do?" she asked, waving wildly, getting Romero's attention. He was making a sandwich in the kitchen and was caught off guard when he saw Jennybell waving him over.

"He's in the law department, let's just say," he told her.

"Give me one moment, please," she said, covering up the phone's speaker to talk to Romero. "This is Mr. Marlongo, one of Sandra's clients. He says he has a very rich friend in the law field who wants to acquire service. I told him we were only dealing with certain clients but he said he highly recommends him."

95

Romero thought for a moment. Mr. Marlongo himself spent four to five hundred dollars a session with Sandra almost each time, now he was recommending a personal friend? He had to make an exception.

"Tell him we'll make an exception just for him," Romero told her to say. Jennybell nodded.

"Mr. Marlongo?" she called.

"Still here."

"Give your friend your card, have him call and set up an appointment."

"Wonderful," he said.

"We're making a one-time exception for you because of your loyal service of the last year," she said.

"Well that's kind of you. I'll take care of everything and you guys should be receiving a call within twenty-four hours," he told her.

"Alright… bye-bye," she said, hanging up.

"You did real well," Romero said, giving her a tap on the rear. Jennybell smiled with crossed arms, proud.

Chapter 12

Taking the last bite out of his Big Mac, Romero wadded the wrapped and tossed it in the waste basket. After sipping the last bit of his soft drink and tossing it away as well, he came over to the motel bathroom and found Juliet. She was applying lip gloss as she prepared to meet her last client of the night.

"You look good, baby… you ready for the main event?" he asked, standing in the doorway.

"Mhmm. So this guy is supposed to be loaded, huh?"

"Somethin' like that. He asked for you so… you know he a thirsty-worsty chasin' a PYT."

"Mhmm… and yo' number one gon' milk his butt like a cow, ain't that right babe?" she said to him with assurance. Juliet turned to him and gave him a hug around the neck.

"That's right," Romero said as he was given a light peck to the lips. "What's all that for?"

"For nothin'," she said only inches from his face. "I love you."

Romero cleared his throat. What he was about to say next had been on his heart but he didn't know when he would say it… it was time now.

"You know I love you, right?"

"Yeah," she answered.

"I'm for real. You know you're my ace? Jennybell and Sandra are my girls and I'd kill for them but you… you got my heart, Juliet. You gots to know that."

There was a pause between them; Romero held her gaze with seriousness and she smiled softly, embracing him tightly.

"I know," she said into the crook of his neck. "I've always known, babe."

Just then there came a knock at the door and both Juliet and Romero knew it was the client. So with one last kiss, she left and closed the door behind her. Going over to the front door she opened it up and met a short, stocky man in a power suit. He was a "silver fox" who was ruggedly handsome. Doing a quick scan, Juliet guessed he was about fifty-five to sixty years old.

"Well hello, Mr. Difano," she smiled, stepping to the side. "Come on in."

"Thank you... Sweet Baby, correct?" he said, stepping inside.

"Sweet as candy, correct." Juliet was dressed in a thin silk mini-dress. She walked seductively past Mr. Difano, leading the way and he eyed her shapely curves. She went to the table and took a seat. "Come sit down," she told him. "Or you can stand... your choice."

He stood.

"So... this is the deal, Mr. Difano. Before we go on further I have to ask... are you a cop?"

He scoffed. "No, far from it," he said.

"Good, then you won't mind showing me your cock?" she said boldly.

He shifted uneasily. "Well... I guess it was bound to come out anyway," he said, undoing his pants. He pulled out his manhood and proved himself. Juliet looked at it and was satisfied. She then stood up and came over to him and gave his limp dick a gentle touch.

"Nice. Gimme one second," she said, going to the bathroom. Mr. Difano was filled with lust and immediately began to undress, but as soon as his pants were down, Romero came out the bathroom.

"Who the hell are you?" Difano asked with caution. He was so caught off guard that he didn't bother to pull up his pants.

"Mr. Difano, my name is Rome and I represent the woman you will be seeing this evening."

"What is this? Some type of shakedown?" he asked.

"Not at all. I just came out to tell you to treat the lady with respect and you'll get what you want. I'll be close by and watching," he told him.

"Well that's good to know, son. Now, if you would be so kind as to get the hell out of here so me and Sweet Baby can continue our little... date, I can pay my bill and drive back to the lighter side of life."

There was an awkward silence between them. Romero had never encountered someone so cocky and disrespectful. "Aight, like I said... be cool and she gon' take care of you," he said, backing up to leave.

When Juliet got the knock on the door, she came out and found

Difano undressing. She had heard everything that was said. "Well aren't we bullheaded," she stated in a sexy tone.

"Little lady, in my line of work you meet tons of slick-talking guys. I pride myself on being able to cut through bullshit." He was sitting on the bed in his t-shirt and boxers. Juliet came and stood in front of him. She didn't like the man's attitude but she had to continue. She was just going to lay it on him to the point he gave his entire wallet over.

"So, Mr. Difano… what do you desire this evening?" she asked seductively.

Difano rubbed his thighs in thought. "Little lady… how 'bout you give me the house special?"

"Mmm, well, Mr. Difano, that's an expensive meal," she informed him.

"Well I'm glad I brought an inch worth of cash," he told her, smiling. Juliet stepped between his legs and allowed her dress to fall to the floor where she stepped out of it. She stood only in her black Victoria's Secret undergarments. She went down to her knees before him and gently pushed Difano onto his back. She rubbed his thighs and pulled down his boxers. She tossed them to the carpet. Taking his semi-hard dick in her hand, Juliet gave his beet-red dickhead a lick. Difano tensed up with shock and a quickening heartbeat. Juliet then took him into her warm, wet mouth fully and began to give him oral copulation.

"Oh God, oh Sweet Baby, it's good," he moaned in pleasure, looking down at her. Juliet sucked his dick like she was auditioning for a porno film. She took her time with him and made sure she cleaned every inch of his shaft with her mouth, and after five minutes, Mr. Difano was ready for sex. "Come on and park it doggy-style, darling," he told her. Juliet climbed on the bed on her hands and knees. Difano wasted no time pushing his hard cock deep into her moist pussy. Juliet's face twisted with pleasure as he gripped her shoulders and began to ram himself in and out of her.

"Ooh," cried Juliet as her body shook from his thrusts.

"Oh yeah, that's it Sweet Baby, cry out for papa," he said through clenched teeth. He reached and grabbed one of Juliet's breasts and pinched her nipple.

"Mmm… oooh, shhhit-yeah," she moaned. Juliet couldn't believe that a man his age was giving it to her so well; she was actually enjoying the sex. Difano slowed his pumps and pulled himself out. He was so horny that he put his face down into Juliet's ass and started rapidly lapping her asshole while finger-fucking her pussy. This sent electrical currents of sexual stimulation all through Juliet's body like never before. She hadn't had a man lick her asshole before. It felt so shockingly good that she could hardly control her breathing.

"Ooo Godddd… ooo goddamn-mmm… yeah," she wept in ecstasy. Difano stopped then and took his cock in hand. He rubbed his cock up and down her ass crack until he stopped at the gate of her brown eye and pushed forward. Juliet took only a split second to realize what was going on and lunged forward. She reached back and blocked him off.

"Oh no, Sweet Baby doesn't do anal, sorry," she told him respectfully. Difano was extremely disappointed and held a surprising look on his face. He couldn't believe this whore was being modest.

"All right," he told her, seemingly complying. Juliet moved her hand and turned back around, but as soon as she did she was tightly grabbed by Difano around her midsection with one hand and felt him forcefully attempting to push himself into her butthole.

"Ah!" she cried out. "No! I said no!"

"C'mere you little slut," he snarled. Juliet became frightened and fell flat on her stomach, clenching her butt cheeks, but when she did that he fell with her and his weight rammed his dick deep inside her anus. Juliet yelled out in pain while Difano moaned out, "Ahh yeah, there it is!"

Juliet's mouth hung wide open in horror as her virgin back door was raped. She was so hurt that she almost forgot protocol for emergencies. Juliet banged the wall to the room next door with an open palm.

*   *   *

Romero was playing Angry Birds on his iPhone when he heard the bangs on the wall. At first he didn't register its meaning because he had never had to respond to it, but seconds after he sprang into action, dashing out and over to the room next door. Romero could hear Juliet's cries as he frantically slid the keycard in the lock. His stomach was in knots as he entered. When the door swung open and he ran in, he found Mr. Difano on top of Juliet; he was steadily pumping inside her and she yelped with every thrust.

"What the fuck?!" Romero said, completely shocked. He rushed over just as Difano himself frantically got up and punched the man hard in the side of his head. Difano went crashing hard into the nightstand, knocking off its contents. Juliet sobbed, quickly curling up into a ball as Romero went to her side. "Baby are you—" Romero began but was abruptly cut off. He was smashed in the head with the desk lamp. He went down onto the bed with a bounce and quickly turned on his back in defense mode. Difano jumped onto him and went for his throat.

"You fucking nigger!" Difano growled.

Juliet was in the corner screaming and crying. Romero's mouth was ajar as he was choked. He held onto the man's wrist, gasping for air as they both slid off the edge of the bed. When they hit the floor, Difano's grip was lost and Romero scrambled to gain a better position. Still naked from the bottom down, Difano rolled onto his back with the condom still on his now-limp dick. He was about to raise up but received a hammer fist to the nose and mouth area. Romero was on top of him and was now pounding his face every clear chance he got. Over and over again he pounded. Blood splattered Romero's knuckles and dress shirt.

"Romey, stop, you'll kill him!" shouted Juliet.

Romero did as she ordered and stopped. He was breathing hard and perspiring. He climbed off the bloody man and stood over him. He held the look of anger and disgust on his face. He looked over at Juliet. "You all right?" he asked aggressively.

Her face was red and wet from tears. She nodded.

"Get yo' shit on, we outta here."

Juliet did as she was told and moved off the bed as fast as her aching body would allow her. "Is he breathing?" she asked, pulling up her panties.

"Get dressed, I don't know!" Romero looked down at the beaten man and saw no rise and fall in his chest. He feared the worst. Moving over to the bathroom, Romero filled up a plastic metal cup full of cold water, came back out, and splashed it in the man's face. The water managed to clear some of the blood from the man's face but failed to even stir him.

"Babe… babe did he wake up?" Juliet asked.

Romero put both his hands behind his head and brought them forward to wipe his face. He felt sick, not because he had killed a man but that he had killed a white man and had done it in a motel room in his name. He had to think, and think fast. Juliet came over and looked down at the dead man with wild eyes. "Oh God… is he?" she said. Romero looked to her.

"Help me wrap him up."

"What? Babe, no."

"Juliet," he snapped low. "This is murder. We have to get him out this room. Now, grab the blanket and help me wrap him up."

Juliet was scared but she did as told. She pulled the blanket off the bed and went to cover him.

"Hold on, take that condom off him," he told her.

"Huh? Why?" she whined.

"Because your pussy DNA is on it! Juliet, woman the fuck up, this is not a test, are you my ace? Are you my bitch?!" he said to her.

"Yes!" she answered harshly.

"Then ride for yo' nigga and stop cryin'."

Juliet swallowed and took a deep breath. She pulled herself together by wiping her tears and following Romero's orders. Minutes later the dead body was wrapped up like a burrito.

"Grab all his shit and take the money he got," Romero told her. She gathered the man's things and found his Coach wallet. When she unzipped it, she pulled out an inch of crispy one hundred dollar bills.

"Romey," Juliet called. He came over and she handed him the cash. Romero thumbed through the bills and made an educated guess.

"This every bit of four to five grand. What else you find?" he asked, pocketing the cash.

"Um… credit cards, pictures… his business card," she said, searching. "California State… Supreme Court, 10th District… Honorable Judge Tomas P. Difano."

Romero's face frowned with confusion. He snatched the card from her and read it to himself. "Oh my fucking God," he said low and in disbelief. He sat down on the bed looking at the card, hoping he wasn't reading what he was reading. But he was. The man he had killed was a judge.

"Babe," Juliet said with worry. "What now?"

Romero shook his head with wide eyes. He was lost. "Just… let me think," he told her calmly. Romero sat and contemplated his next move. Everything was all bad and he had no true way out. The only thing he could think about was "dump him," get him out this room and dump him.

"Aight, I know what to do," he said, standing up.

*   *   *

Under the cover of night, Romero drove Difano in his car to a remote location on the outskirts. Juliet followed him in his 300. Once they were out there, they dressed and placed Difano in the driver's seat, then wiped the car down, getting rid of any of their prints. After they were done, they returned to the motel with cleaning supplies and a UV glow light for blood inspection. Romero was thinking smart and used all the free knowledge he gained from C.S.I, Law and Order, and The First 48. From top to bottom he and Juliet cleaned the room of any signs of blood, then when they were done they gathered all signs that ever led to them being there and put it in the trunk of the car. Romero then turned in both keys to the rooms to the motel desk clerk.

When they got back to the apartment, Juliet went straight to the shower in the master bedroom. She said nothing to Sandra and Jennybell who tried speaking to her. Romero tossed his car keys on the kitchen counter and rested with his head down on it for a moment.

"Rome, is something the matter?" Sandra asked from the living room couch. Jennybell was on the floor watching cable but looked to Romero as well with concern. Romero stood upright and came into the living room cross section which led to the back rooms. He stopped for a moment. He looked tired.

"Everything fine," he lied. "I shut down the rooms over at Lucky's… 'mma find a new spot, better spot… don't ask questions." Sandra and Jennybell frowned.

"Oookay… well what's wrong with Juliet?" asked Sandra.

"She coo', just tired is all, don't trip over her," he told them, waving his hand towards the back rooms.

"So, how'd it go with that new client?" asked Jennybell. Romero hesitated. He didn't want to tell them the truth just yet, if at all, so he lied again.

"Oh he was loaded, paid a nice piece," he smiled weak and fake. There was an awkward pause after that. Jennybell went back to watching TV, Sandra eyed Romero and he stood uneasy.

"'mma hit the bed, 'm dog tired, so…"

"All right, baby, go get some rest," Sandra told him softly.

103

Romero nodded and left. When he entered his bedroom, he could hear the shower going. He kicked off his shoes, pulled off his shirt and slipped out his jeans. He went to the bathroom and could hear light sobs coming from inside. He entered the steam-filled room and could see Juliet's naked figure through the opaque glass. When he opened the glass door, she flinched. Even though she was wet he could see that she was crying by the distraught look on her face. Romero stepped in after stepping out of his boxers and when he did, she immediately embraced him tightly and began to cry harder.

"Shhh," he cooed. "Be coo'. You all right now, shhh."

She cried as a release of all the hurt she was feeling, mentally, emotionally, spiritually, and physically. She started kissing him and he started kissing her back.

"Make love to me, Rome, please make love to me," she said between kisses. And he obliged her.

Chapter 13

"What we got here?" Homicide detective John Rola asked as he approached the crime scene.

"DOA, white male, looks to be approximately fifty-five to sixty-five years of age," the young patrolman reported.

"Who touch my crime scene?"

"No one, sir. Coroner there has been waiting and CSU is on standby as well."

"Good work, officer…?"

"Meyers, sir."

"Good work, Meyers. I'll take it from here," Rola said, pulling on latex gloves. He went under the yellow tape and waved over one CSU worker and the coroner. The dead victim sat stiff with his head back and mouth slightly ajar. His face was badly beaten and covered in blood that had dried.

"Poor bastard," Rola mumbled. "All right… you two follow my lead and do your thing step by step as I finish each area." The two understood. Rola stepped up to the black BMW and reached into the open window. He found the victim's wallet inside his suit pocket. When he stepped back, he allowed CSU to dust for prints and the coroner to examine the body. Detective Rola carefully searched the wallet and found the victim's ID. He read that the man's name was Tomas Difano. Rola felt he recognized the name, and once he searched further he found a business card that told him everything.

"Jesus… he's a Supreme Court judge," he mumbled with dismay. Rola could see the shitstorm that would hit the media. Continuing his search, he found photos of what could only be his family; wife and kids. Rola hated breaking bad news to the victims' families, but over the ten years he had been in homicide, he had grown a sort of thick skin to grief. Rola looked around at the area and squinted from the noon sun. There was nothing in the crime area as far as civilization. Someone had to dump the victim out there.

"What's the cause, doc?" Rola asked, carefully handing over the wallet to the CSU member.

"He was beaten to death from what I can tell. There's blunt force trauma to his face and head area. This man seems well into his late fifties so I wouldn't be surprised if the actual cause of death was a heart attack," the female reported. She looked good, Rola thought. She could pass as a real fox if she lost the baggy uniform and put on some makeup.

"You got a time of death?" he asked.

"Judging from rigor… I'd say he died anywhere between one a.m. and two a.m. I'd have to get him downtown to my office to be sure." Rola nodded and stepped over to the CSI.

"What did you lift?"

"Got a few partials but that's it so far. Car looks to have been wiped down. There's signs of cleaning agent residue," the geeky man explained.

"All right, let's pop the trunk," said Rola, going over to remove the key from the ignition. As he did, he noticed the victim's pants were undone and his dress shoes were untied. In fact he saw that all the man's clothes looked in disarray. What the hell were you doing way out here? Rola asked himself. Upon opening the trunk, there was nothing to be noticed out of the ordinary. It was a spare tire located inside the floor and some random tools. There also was a suitcase. It was nice; one of those golden-lock leather-bound briefcases that looked like it came from European lands. When Rola pushed the lock triggers to the sides, surprisingly it opened. Inside were some interesting items. Rola whistled with wide eyes.

"Somebody's hiding a stash," he said. There were a few pornographic magazines. "Barely Legal," "Just 18," "19 and Nasty," and "Tight." There was also a small bottle of petroleum jelly inside.

"Judge Difano, you horny, horny old goat, you," Rola said low as he flipped quickly through one of the book's pages. There was nothing else inside the case once he was done, so he turned everything over to the clean-up team and told them to contact him once they ran their checks. He had to drive out to the hills to inform Difano's family, and maybe gather more clues as to what the hell happened and who the hell had done it.

*   *   *

Tomas Difano lived in a high-class neighborhood in the rich part of Long Beach. Rola marveled at all the mini-mansions with their three carport garages and gated properties. Once he found the judge's home, it was no different and he had to be buzzed in from the gate after he explained who he was and what his visit was concerning. Pulling up and around the circle driveway, he noticed an older woman standing in wait at the front door. He parked and got out.

"Mrs. Difano, I presume," he said, coming up on the small silver-headed woman and shaking her soft hand. John Rola towered over the woman because he was naturally tall, 6'3", in fact. He was what women looked for. He was tall, dark, and handsome. Back when he was a rookie, the squad used to call him "PBF," or Pretty Boy Floyd.

"What's this visit about, Mr. Rola?" she asked.

He swallowed and cleared his throat. "Can we step inside? Maybe have a seat, Mrs.—"

"Sure," she cut in, "as soon as you tell me what your business is here."

Rola nodded in agreement. "Well, ma'am… I'm sad to report to you that around eleven this morning, a patrolman found your husband inside his vehicle, he was deceased… coroner feels he may have been killed from blunt force trauma to the head which may have led to a heart attack."

Mrs. Difano looked unfazed, unfazed but with eyes that looked saddened.

"I'm sorry for your loss, but—"

"Would you like to come in, Mr. Rola?" she cut in again.

"Uh, sure," he told her. He followed her through the large house until they entered the living room. She took a seat in a nice flower chair and motioned to the couch for him. Rola took a seat.

"Mrs. Difano, did your husband have any known enemies that you know or any threatening phone calls or anything like that?" he asked.

"Where did you find him?"

"Uh… he was on the outskirts of the city, the lower south end," he told her.

She scoffed with dead eyes. "He loved his whores."

"Excuse me?"

"I've known for years… never could catch the son of a bitch, but I knew. Now he's dead… dead because he loved his whores more than me." A single tear fell from her eye and rolled down her cheek. She wiped it away quickly. She continued, "I wasn't in love with him anymore, hadn't been for years… I just played along like a good judge's wife… who would take me if I

107

divorced him? A fifty-eight-year-old woman on her own."

"Mrs. Difano, have you ever seen him with any of his whores as you say?" he asked.

"I told you no… he was very busy, very private. He'd come home, we'd eat, chit-chat, and he'd go into his study until bedtime."

Rola nodded. "Okay… I'd like to possibly look in your husband's study, check for anything that may help me in my investigation. With your permission, of course."

"I don't care, be my guest… I have to call my children. They're going to be devastated," she said with that same blank look.

"You'll also have to come downtown and identify the body. I can accompany you down after you make the calls you need."

"Thank you… that'll be fine. His study is the first room in the front hall," she told him, rising up.

Difano's study was impressive. It was nicely furnished with cherry oak wood and tight leather furniture. It reminded him of an actual judge's chambers at a courthouse. Pictures of the late judge with people of power lined the walls and shelves, certificates and plaques of merit as well. Rola came around the desk and fished through pointless documents. He took a seat and did the same with the drawers and got the same results. He then turned to Difano's laptop and turned it on. It took seconds to boot and came to the main screen. Rola searched through files and at first came up with nothing, then he saw a file labeled PYT and clicked on it. The screen lit up with hundreds of mini-photo icons. Rola clicked one and it was a photo of a young girl giving a man a blowjob. He clicked through more and got the same thing… smut, hardcore, and young. Rola started to feel that the judge was a pervert, but aside from that, he didn't have anything to lead Rola further along. Turning the computer off and sitting for a moment, he saw something that he overlooked on the desk. He reached and picked up a card. The car had red lips on it and a number on the back. Rola frowned, looking from its front to its back. He picked up the landline phone that sat on the desk and just before he dialed the card he thought about "star 69" so he dialed it and waited. Moments later a man answered.

"Judge Difano, good afternoon. I trust the appointment went well last night?" Rola thought fast.

"Mhmm," he answered curiously.

"Good, good. Maybe now you could pass my name along to some of your friends at Cole, Steinberg, and Walte," the man said. Rola froze. He didn't know if he could continue to play this role. He tried though…

"Name, son?" Rola said, doing his best old man voice.

"Terry, sir… Terry Marlongo."

Rola found a pen and wrote the name down.

"Judge Difano? …who is this?" asked Marlongo.

"This is Detective John Rola of the LBPD, sir. I'd like to speak with you further about—" But the line went dead. Rola hung up the phone and pocketed the name and card. He was getting somewhere now.

It was now half past ten at night and Detective John Rola's day still wasn't over. He had spent most of his day doing press interviews and report papers. The media was on fire with his case and it was the top story. Now John sat behind his desk under the soft glow of his lamp going over the case file which held the coroner's and CSU report on the evidence they may or may not have found. All was quiet in the office because most of the precinct had gone home for the night. Only a couple of late-night workers remained in homicide.

Who murdered Tomas Difano? was the question to answer. When Rola pieced together the evidence at hand, he found that Difano slummed on the down-low with women of the night and was into young girls. The day before he was murdered, he was contacted by a man named Terry Marlongo who Rola found out through his sources was a paralegal at a small firm. Marlongo clearly hooked Difano up with whoever he was with and expected a favor in return. Rola hadn't made it out to Marlongo's place of residence but it was first on his to-do list. Next came the red lip calling card. Forensics had run the prints and besides his own prints and Difano's, there was a useless partial and one visible.

Rola scanned and uploaded the print into the system and after zooming through thousands of print profiles, it found a match.

"Well-well-well, hello little lady," Rola mumbled as he came closer to the computer screen and took hold of the mouse. Her name was Juliet E. Witmore, age currently approaching eighteen years old. She was 5'4", 129 pounds, blonde, and her last known address was in the state of Idaho. She was arrested for failing to appear due to a traffic warrant back in 2011.

Besides that she was clean.

"What the hell are you doing in California?" Rola asked himself low. He tried to call her last known number but found that it was disconnected, so he went online to see if she had a Facebook page and surprisingly she didn't. "What eighteen-year-old girl in America doesn't have a Facebook?" he said, puzzled. He then picked up his desk phone and the red lip calling card and dialed Star 67 to block his number, then dialed the number on the card. The number just rang and rang, and had no voicemail service. Hanging up, Detective Rola sat back in his chair and rubbed his face. He was tired and needed to go home and rest. He printed Juliet Witmore's mug shot and placed it in his case file. He was even closer to finding out what happened to his victim.

*   *   *

"Happy birthday!" the group of waiters shouted with glee after completing the full song. Juliet blew out the flame on her number 18 birthday candle and everyone applauded. Romero wanted to escape Long Beach for a few days so he took the girls to Las Vegas. They stayed in the Mirage Hotel, the secret garden of Siegfried and Roy. The city was a sight for anyone of any age to see at night; it sparkled from entrance to exit with brilliant lights and dazzling hotels. Like always, on their first day in Sin City, the girls wanted to sightsee, so they—along with Romero—drove around town going to the Las Vegas National History Museum, Meadows Mall, and the Boulevard Mall. The whole time Romero had plans to surprise Juliet with a nice dinner. She was so modest that she didn't even mention it to anyone. Romero believed that she probably would have let it pass uncelebrated. They dined downstairs in their hotel's restaurant called Rasinto's. It was packed wall to wall with happy patrons.

"Ooh, you guys are so crazy," Juliet said while blushing as the waiters individually said happy birthday and went back to work.

"You guys?" Jennybell said, confused. "Girl this was a surprise for me as well. Romey must have done this… or Sandra."

"Wasn't me either," Sandra said, looking to Romero.

"I couldn't allow you to just get off without some cake and ice cream," he smiled. Juliet smiled back.

"Girl, what you wish for?" asked Jennybell.

"She can't say or it won't come true," added Sandra.

"My wish already came true," said Juliet with fixed eyes on Romero. He didn't know what she meant but he was glad she had whatever came true.

After the cake and ice cream, the three of them strolled the city until they came across a place called Kinks and Cuffs. It was an adult accessory store. The girls were overjoyed to go in and Romero just followed their lead without complaint. Browsing through the shop, they saw all sorts of sexual toys, tools, books, clothes, and DVDs. It was like no other place Romero had ever been. Yes there were porno stores around his area back in Chicago, but none so large and so populated.

"Girl, look at this thing here," Jennybell told Sandra and Juliet. It was a twelve-inch double-sided dildo.

"Mm… wow, that's dangerous right there," Juliet said, taking it and looking it over.

"Yeah, but it could also be fun. I know Rome would like it, with his freaky ass," said Jennybell.   "Rome'll like what?" he said, coming around the corner. He saw the girls huddled up looking at something.

"This right here," Jennybell said, showing him. Romero took the dildo and gawked.

"Damn… this thing is crazy. Hell yeah, I like it. Who wanna get it and put on a show?" he asked, teasing.

Juliet took it from him and smacked her lips. "Gimme this thing," she giggled. She went silent just for a second. "You really would want to see this in action?"

"Hell yeah, why? …Come on now, what up? You look like you might be in deep thought."

Juliet looked to Sandra… and she rolled her eyes, nodding with a small smile, then she turned to Jennybell and she nodded as well. "Aight, let's do it," Juliet said.

*   *   *

When the four of them got back to their hotel room, which was on the seventeenth floor, Romero cracked open a bottle of Moët and rolled a fat blunt. They all sipped and got tipsy and smoked and got high. After a while of bullshitting around, things started to heat up. Sandra brought a chair over in front of the large custom-built bed for Romero sit in. Then the girls all got on the bed and started kissing and touching and taking each other's clothes off.

Romero didn't interfere but he did get undressed down to his black boxer briefs. When the dildo finally came out, Romero was ready for action. Sandra was the "insert woman" and Jennybell and Juliet were the "takers." Romero watched as Sandra carefully slid the large toy inside one, and did the same with the next. Jennybell and Juliet looked like they were linked through their asses. Then, slowly, they started moving their bodies back and forth, back and forth, slow and deep. Each woman moaning softly with pleasure-filled faces as they engulfed their six inches each of fake dick. Romero was hard up. He wanted to join. So he stood up, pulled down his boxer briefs, came over in front of Juliet and stuck his dick in her mouth.

"Sandra baby, go over and get that pussy licked," he told her. She did as told. Now they were all getting pleased, and the world seemed like the best place in the galaxy. Romero watched as Juliet sucked his dick well and rubbed her short hair.

"Ahhh-damn… shhhit, mmm… happy birthday, baby."

She acknowledged him by saying, "Mmm-mmhmm."

Chapter 14

"Mama, help me!" the loud ghostly voice yelled inside Romero's mind as he dreamed. His eyes popped open in the darkness and all he could see was high ceiling. His heart was beating faster than normal and he was slightly irritated that he was awakened by such a pointless and stupid dream. It was West-Coast Red screaming for life just before he was snuffed out. Crazy thing was the voice of the dead pimp came from the mouth of Judge Tomas Difano.

Romero's arms were wrapped around the shoulders of Juliet and Sandra as they slept peacefully on his chest. Jennybell was supposed to have been sleeping between his legs on his lower abdomen but she wasn't there. Slowly and carefully, Romero got up and gently scooted to the edge of the large bed. He sat completely naked and yawned with outstretched arms. His eyes began to adjust to the darkness and he got up and located his boxer briefs and t-shirt. When he was dressed, he walked the soft carpeted floor quietly to the bathroom. When he approached it, he could hear the sink water running. Jennybell, he thought. She always ran the sink water when in the restroom. Romero knew that the swanky hotel suite came equipped with two types of toilets—regular and a bidet. He had to piss so he just let himself in. When the door came open, Romero found Jennybell sitting on the toilet's closed top. She was slumped with one of her legs crossed like a male and tied tightly around her ankle was her pink belt. Sticking out from between her big toe was a needle. Romero was perplexed for a moment and what he was seeing didn't register at first. Jennybell turned to look at him slowly with very low, dreamy eyes that seemed glossy. Romero looked at the sink and saw a burnt spoon, tinfoil pieces, and a lighter.

"Romey... Romey, please don't get mad at me," she said, slurring her words. Romero was stuck; he just held a look of confusion. "Babe, I just... I just was, um, ummmm?" she slurred out.

Romero had to remain cool, he couldn't lose it, even though he could and should... he had to keep his cool and be a boss. "Bitch, you broke the house rule. Don't do drugs unless the king allows it. Bitch, you gots to pay, so finish up and bring ya funky ass on out."

Jennybell tried to say something but he just slammed the door on her. From there he went over and cut on the lights and got dressed. He then set up his chair in the living room with three stools in front of him. From there, he went into the bedroom and woke both the girls and told them sternly, "Get up now. Family meeting."

Romero sat with a stone face and hands folded in his lap. He only had to wait a few minutes until Juliet and Sandra tiptoed out of the bedroom dressed only in their t-shirts and panties, both of them looked tired as they took their seats. Moments later, Jennybell emerged from the bathroom dressed the same. She looked tired as well but Romero knew it was for a different reason.

"I'll get straight to the point. If one of you girls breaks the house rules, what should the punishment be? Juliet?" he asked, serious.

She shrugged. "Depends on the house rule, I'd say," she told him.

"Aight, Sandra?" he asked.

"Um... I agree," she told him.

"Jennybell?" he asked as well.

"Me too, I agree," she said low.

"All right, let's say I caught one of you doing drugs. Cocaine or heroin? What do you think I would do?" He looked at Juliet.

"Those drugs? Uh... beat that girl or put her out the family?" she said. He looked to Sandra next.

"I'd want to beat her but maybe put her on some type of punishment or strict probation?" she told him. Romero nodded, then looked to Jennybell.

"I agree," she simply said with a soft voice.

"All right, well... it's been brought to my attention that one of you has been lying to the king. One of you has been getting high on something other than the allowed weed. All of you stated that the person should be at the very least... be physically chastised, so... do you all agree to me carrying out this punishment justly?" he asked them all. There was silence for a few moments; the girls were worried and confused.

"I agree one hundred percent," Juliet answered first.

"Me too," said Sandra.

"Yes," added Jennybell looking him dead in the eyes.

"Then it's settled... Jennybell, front and center, bitch," he said

114

powerfully.

Juliet and Sandra were shocked but relieved at the same time that it wasn't one of them. Jennybell got up and stood in front of Romero. She looked sad and high.

"I don't do hardcore drugs and none of my queens do whatever that shit was I caught you doing stops right now or you're out this kingdom, banished back to the slums. Understand me?"

"Yes," she said low with watering eyes.

"Yes what?!" he said loudly, making all the girls flinch.

"Yes, my king," she said as teardrops ran down both cheeks.

Romero felt sympathy but showed none. "Now, not only did you disrespect me, you disrespected your sisters who trusted you to do right by me… and for that… they too will punish you, hear me?"

"Y-yes… my king," she said with more leaking tears.

Juliet and Sandra frowned. They looked at one another in puzzlement. Romero stood up and faced Jennybell head on.

"Sandra," he called. "Come to me." She did but was uneasy in doing so. She came to him and he placed her in front of Jennybell.

"Baby girl," he said softly. "Obey me… you're gonna smack the shit out of her one good time and tell her what she shouldn't have done, aight?"

Looking into Jennybell's teary eyes, Sandra was sick. She had never hurt anyone on purpose. Now she had to smack her friend. Sandra closed her eyes and took a deep breath. "All right," she told Romero. He took a step back and Sandra raised her hand up and to the side. "You don't use drugs in this family… you were bogus, Jenny." Sandra came across her face hard and the smack sounded like a ruler hitting a bad child's thigh times ten. Jennybell shrieked with a turning head. She stumbled backwards a step.

"Now apologize to her," he said.

"I'm-I'm sorry, my queen-sister," she said, holding her hot face and crying softly.

Romero took Sandra by her shoulder and embraced her from the back and kissed her on the cheek. She then went back to her stool.

"Juliet," he called next. She got up and knew what she had to do. So when she came over and faced Jennybell, she wasted no time.

"You used drugs and that's a no-no in this house. You were wrong, Jenny." Juliet's arm went up and to the side then came down hard across the

115

already tender left side of Jennybell's face. She shrieked even louder and stumbled backwards that time. She was sobbing now. Romero hugged and kissed Juliet, sending her back to her stool.

"Get into place," he told Jennybell, "and stop all that crying, you wasn't cryin' when you know you was breaking me and yo' sisters' hearts by shootin' drugs between ya fuckin' toes," he said viciously down at her. But Jennybell couldn't help it; she cried until she was back in front of him.

"Now... are you ready?" he asked. Through tears and a twisted face that was wet and red, she put her hands down and nodded her head. But surprisingly, instead of a smack, Romero gave her a quick and powerful gut shot which knocked the wind out of her and sent her flopping to the floor. Juliet and Sandra both looked shocked and nauseated, both covered their mouths and Jennybell gasped for air while rocking in a fetal position. Romero, on the inside was sad he had to do what he did, but he also knew that doing what he did was showing strength that he wasn't a complete pushover.

"Never disrespect this kingdom again, next your ass is out," he said down to her as he stepped over her. He came to Juliet and Sandra and told them to come back to bed with him. "You sleep on the couch."

The three retired to the bedroom. Jennybell was in so much pain she couldn't let a sound escape her mouth, but when she could she simply whispered, "I'm sorry."

*　　*　　　*

Even though it was 6:30 in the morning, Detective John Rola didn't care about appropriate times when he needed to speak with homicide witnesses or victims' families, he just came when he came. He drove his unmarked car—which was a newish 2011 Dodge Charger—out to Cherry Hills. The hills were middle class homes with a low-crime rate to the area. Rola turned down Windsor Road until he found the house he was looking for. When he pulled to the curb around seven a.m., he saw a woman escorting a small child onto a small yellow school bus. He figured it was Terry Marlongo's kid and wife. Dressed in casual clothing, Rola got out of his car and got the woman's attention as she headed back up her driveway.

"Excuse me, ma'am."

"Yes?" the woman said with caution. She saw his badge and sidearm on his waist. "Can I help you?"

"Maybe. I'm looking for Terry Marlongo. Is this his residence?" he asked politely.

"He's my husband," she told him simply.

"Oh, that's great. Is your husband in, Mrs. Marlongo?"

"Yes, he's in. What's this concerning?"

"Oh, Mr. Marlongo's name came up in one of my cases and I just wanted to speak with him to see if he could possibly help me along in my investigation."

"And what's that?" she asked.

"That's confidential, I'm afraid," he told her.

"Hmm, and what's your name?" she asked, curious.

"John Rola, ma'am, Detective John Rola."

"Well, Detective, follow me on up, Terry's getting ready for work."

They went into the house and she told Rola to wait in the foyer. She called upstairs to her husband and moments later he came down the steps. Terry Marlongo was a thin man who looked to be in his mid-thirties. He put Rola in the mind of Mr. Rogers only younger and better dressed.

"Terry, this is Detective Rola and he says he needs to speak with you about one of his cases," his wife told him. Terry made eye contact with Rola and was just as confused as his wife was.

"I'm sure it's nothing, honey. How may I help you, Detective?" he asked, coming over to Rola.

"Can we speak in private?"

"You can speak in front of my wife," he told Rola with smug confidence.

"All right… Judge Tomas Difano, you spoke to him not two days ago, right?"

"Correct, he's a close acquaintance of mine."

"Well, I don't know if you've caught the news but he was found dead in his car yesterday morning." Marlongo frowned and his wife gasped. "I called you yesterday and you—"

"Oh yes," he cut in. "Yes, um… yes that was… a misunderstanding. Maybe we could speak in private. Honey, will you excuse us please?" Mr. Marlongo pulled open double doors that led to an office. Rola went in and the doors were closed behind them. "Jesus Christ… Tomas Difano is dead?"

Marlongo said with disbelief as he went over to his desk.

"Murdered, actually," Rola corrected him. "Tell me about this." Rola went inside his folder and presented him with the lip print business card. Terry seemed to go blank when he looked upon the card.

"What's that?" he asked with a bluff.

"Mr. Marlongo, please... don't waste my time. You know what it is. Now, tell me, who did you hook the judge up with for sex? And what does this card have to do with it?"

Terry clenched his teeth, flexing his jaw muscles. He couldn't believe what was going on. He took a deep breath and prepared himself. "I can't let this get back to my wife," he said.

"Tell me what I want to know and she'll never hear it from me," Rola promised.

"All right... there's this service... it's a sort of dating service—"

"You mean illegal prostitution service," Rola cut in.

"Shh," Marlongo cautioned. "Whatever... anyways, this service caters to only those higher-ups, and Difano mentioned he wanted... you know... a release of sorts. So, I simply called in a favor, got the okay, and passed the car onto him. That's all."

"Do you know the names of any of the women from this service?" Rola asked, taking notes.

"Yeah, there are three girls I believe. Uh... Baby Girl, Sweet Baby, and uh... Sweet Thing? I think."

"Does the name Juliet Witmore ring a bell?" Rola asked.

"No," he said, shaking his head slightly.

"She's blonde, about seventeen to eighteen years old? Here... take a look," Rola said, pulling out the mug shot and hanging it to him. Marlongo eyed the paper and nodded, handing it back.

"Yeah, that's Sweet Baby. That's who I recommended, but I don't know if he actually chose her," he told Rola.

"Mr. Warlongo—"

"Marlongo," he corrected him.

"Whatever, listen, with this new information, I'm going to need you to further participate in a sting operation to apprehend this woman—"

"No," Marlongo objected. "I can't be associated with something of this nature. My wife and career's on the line, I—"

"You will or I'll build a case against you as well," Rola cut back in, threatening. "Mr. Marlongo, this is no game, a man has been murdered and you are the only person able to lead us to the prime suspect. Listen, all you have to do is make the appointment and show up. When whatever type of deal's struck, then my team'll swoop in and take care of the rest. After that, you can go home and continue to pull the wool over your wife's eyes."

Mr. Marlongo sighed and placed his hands on his hips. He then shook his head in defeat and smacked his lips. "All right, okay… as long as this stays quite on my part," Marlongo agreed.

Rola nodded and pulled his cell off his hip. He needed to call into his chief to see if he could get the okay for his operation plan. He was son his way to possibly bursting the case wide open.

   *   *   *

It was a silent morning in Vegas when the four were gathering their things to leave, and even a quieter long ride back to Long Beach. When they got back to the apartment, it was awkward. Sandra went to her room, Romero went out onto the balcony, Jennybell went into her room, and Juliet stood in the living room as though she was divided.

Romero sat over a dozen stories high in deep thought. The city looked beautiful as always and the sun was out but was not as hot. He slouched holding a large blunt between his fingertips. Bringing it to his lips, he puffed deep and held the week smoke in his lungs. Romero was still messed up about catching Jennybell injecting whatever drugs into her foot. Things were crazy, his life was crazy. He was a pimp, plain and simple. He even felt like one, giving orders, collecting cash from girls who sold themselves for money. He was supposed to have stopped when he reached one hundred thousand but he was well past that. He hadn't written his book for months and it bothered him, even though he was making money without complaint, it still bothered him. He had to come up with an exit plan… and soon.

Minutes later, the sliding door on the balcony came open. Juliet came around in front of him and squatted down. With hands on thighs she looked into his eyes. "Baby, she's really sorry… I just came from talking to her and she's sad thinking that you hate her now," Juliet told him. Romero said nothing, he just smoked on his week and played boss. Juliet smacked her lips and continued. "Look, she wants to talk to you… she's standing in the living room waiting. Give her a chance to explain fully… please, for me."

Romero's tough act melted away and he smiled warmly down at her. Juliet smiled back. He sighed.

"Aight, just for you… send her out," he told her.

"Thank you, baby," she said, rising and giving him a kiss to the lips. Seconds later, Jennybell came out and stood in front of him. She wore a small white tank-top and blue striped pajama bottoms. Jennybell's eyes were sad but she did her best to smile softly. Romero took one last puff of his blunt and tossed the rest over the ledge.

"Speak," he simply said. She began.

"Rome, I'm sorry for doing drugs and breaking the rules and breaking everybody's trust. I'm not a junkie or dopehead… it's just… when I was with Red, he made all his girls shoot dope to keep us dependant on him. I never wanted to do it but once he forced me… I was kinda hooked. When I joined you guys I was going cold turkey, and for a while I could manage. But some nights… some nights those old cravings come back and I lose the battle. I can stop. I will stop. I love being here and I love my sisters and I love you to death. It killed me to see you hurt like you were. I hated that my actions made you and the girls hit me… I know you didn't want to. Rome… forgive me, I don't want you to hate me." She shrugged. "That's it."

Romero nodded and exhaled. "I don't hate you, Jennybell… and you're forgiven, but… you are on probation until I feel you redeemed yourself. No cell phone and no shopping. You will be restricted from using the bathroom behind closed doors and that goes for all occasions, and for your bedroom as well. Got dat?"

"Got it," she said, nodding with a wide grin. "Can I have a hug now?"

Romero opened his arms and she came to him happily and sat on his lap and embraced him. She gave him a kiss to the lips and just for a few seconds it went into a deep Frencher.

"Aight-aight-aight," he told her. "Get off me."

Jennybell stood up in front of him. She was still grinning.

"Turn the Batphone on and y'all get ready for calls. It's… one o'clock now, so… book clients till midnight. We been missin' some good money," he told her.

Jennybell skipped off happily back into the apartment. When she was gone, Romero went back into deep thought. He wondered—like he had been doing since it happened—about that judge he killed and if his body was found yet. Romero hadn't watched the news since the morning before Vegas. He told himself he would catch the local news at three o'clock. He still hadn't told the other girls and neither did Juliet; in fact, they hadn't even spoken about it since that day.

Romero hoped he left no clues, he hoped he got away clean and the police would have to run the case cold. But the thing about hope is… hopes are dashed every day, no day is more special than the next. Police were smart, he knew this… he just hoped for the best and prepared for the worst.

Chapter 15

Romero had chosen the Hilton Hotel not four blocks from the apartment. He rented out two suites next door to one another that had connecting doors between them. Just like before he used one for clients and the other to sit in while he waited for the shift to end. Romero, along with Sandra and Jennybell, were in one room while Juliet prepared herself for the last client on her shift. It was eleven o'clock and the work day was riper than ever. Sandra and Jennybell were already done and had pulled in over $1,500. Jennybell of course put in hard work to please Romero and brought in most. As Romero sat with his legs kicked up and crossed on the bed, the Batphone rang on the desk next to him. He stopped counting his money, turned the television down and motioned to Sandra to answer it.

"Hello, this is Baby Girl, how may I please—" she answered in a sweet voice. "Oh hello, Mr. Marlongo."

Romero listened intently because Mr. Marlongo was the man who hooked the dead judge up with Juliet. When he called to book an appointment earlier, Juliet found Romero and placed him on speaker phone. Mr. Marlongo seemed unaffected by the death of his associate. In fact, he had informed them that he had been out of the country on business and "trusted" that they were well pleased with the compensation Judge Difano should have gave them. Romero didn't speak but was sort of hesitant to take his business. But when Mr. Marlongo inquired about an all-nighter, Romero mimed for her to accept his business. Mr. Marlongo wanted to know where they were rendezvousing but Romero hadn't picked a location. He felt that the reason for his call now was to finally find out so he could head over. Romero listened to Sandra.

"Your date is waiting at the Hilton Suites Hotel, tenth floor, room A-46. Uh-huh... Correct... All right, she'll see you in thirty minutes to an hour."

When Sandra hung up, she was about to go next door and alert Juliet but Romero went instead. When he came into the room through the adjoining doors, he found Juliet naked and drying off. She had just gotten out of the shower and was sitting on the edge of the bed.

"Hey babe, one more and we can go home. I'm actually starving," she told him. Romero came in front of her and leaned against the dresser.

"You getting' thick too, I been noticing," he told her. Juliet's eyes widened and she stood up with a smile. She twisted her body trying to see what he saw.

"You think so? I guess my body is getting fatter, but you like that huh?"

"You know I do. More for the pushin' when I'm hittin' it from the back. More to grab," he told her.

"My boobs, too," she added.

"Oh yeah-yeah, no doubt. Them things plump as well."

Juliet blushed and sat back down, finishing drying off. She liked being labeled "thick." Even though she had a long way to go as far as the "thick" Romero liked, she still loved to hear him say she was. But she was thickening up for reasons beyond her control. She was harboring a secret ever since the New York trip... She was pregnant. Juliet expected she had to be a month and a few days because she hadn't had her period in over a month. She could feel a change in her body and wanted desperately to tell Romero but she was afraid that the timing was all wrong. Juliet hated keeping things from him though; it ate her up to hold it to herself.

"Listen," he began. "Your last client just called and confirmed his arrival. He said he'd be here in thirty to an hour," he told her.

"All right, I'll be ready. Oh, here," Juliet said, getting up wrapped in her towel. She retrieved a wad of money out of the nightstand and brought it to him. "That's like six hundred or so... slow night, sorry."

Romero reached for the money, and when he did he held her hand softly. Juliet was confused but smiled warmly, saying, "What?"

Romero was once again feeling a certain way. He didn't know what was coming over him but he felt soft... he felt done. "You're so good to me, you know that?" he said down to her.

Juliet blushed but was secure in doing so. "What's wrong, babe?" she gently asked.

"I don't know..." he said sadly, confused himself.

"I'm pregnant," she uttered suddenly.

Romero seemed to instantly snap back to reality. Did he hear right?

They were still holding hands. "What you say?" he asked, puzzled.

"I'm... pregnant... I think," she repeated.

"You think? Or are you?"

"Well... I'm almost four and a half weeks over," she explained.

Romero took the money from her and placed it on the dresser top beside him. He then opened her towel and let it drop to the carpet below. Juliet didn't say a word, she just watched him look down upon her flat stomach in thought. Romero went to a bending knee and placed his hands on her hips and slowly gave her stomach a light kiss. "My baby in there?" he said softly, looking into her big blue eyes.

Juliet nodded with a smile.

Romero hugged her midsection with his head on her stomach. Juliet was beyond happy that he was not mad or displeased. She bent over and hugged him back and kissed the top of his head.

    *   *   *

Detective John Rola and his five-man tactical team were dressed in plain clothes as they rode the Hilton elevator to the tenth floor. Their informant—Mr. Terry Marlongo—was stationed downstairs in the parking lot in his car. He wore a wireless tap and was told to wait for their okay to proceed. Detective Rola was given more information and relayed it to his team. Marlongo told him that there would possibly be a male present, a pimp of sorts. Rola also found out that the young woman known as Sweet Baby was doing business out of an inn called Lucky Nights. Rola had plans to execute a search of whatever room or rooms the girl and her pimp used to see if there were traces of possible blood left behind. The coroner's report mentioned that the body of Tomas Difano had been moved after death. When the tactical team reached the tenth floor and went to the A sector, they split up into groups. The mark was said to be located in room A-46 and so Rola and his undercover team simply occupied conjoined rooms across the hall. Rola and a female detective named Nancy Washington entered the room A-53 which was directly across the hall. Minutes later three more plain-dressed officers entered the room A-52. When the knock came to the door which divided them, the team began to undress and redress in tactical gear. Rola had informed the manager of the hotel that he had a warrant for a seizure. After going over a few preliminaries to acquire their rooms and the keycard to room A-46, he also had the clean-up staff on standby for afterwards.

Once everything was set up and all officers were ready, Rola called down to Marlongo and gave him the go ahead. Detective Rola stood at the door looking through the peephole.

* * *

"Wow, pregnant? I'm so jealous." Jennybell pouted as she touched Juliet's stomach.

"I'm gonna be a stepmom," added Sandra. They were all in the waiting suite giving congratulations to Romero and Juliet.

"As of right now she is on maternity leave, no queen of mine will work while she pregnant with my seed. So, to please this client that's coming, because he's a high roller… I'm gonna need both you girls to take care of Mr. Marlongo," Romero told them.

Sandra and Jennybell were surprised. They never handled a client together, none of them had.

"Two for the price of one? …Girl, that baby ain't even here, you sure you pregnant?" Jennybell teased.

"Don't trip, 'mma still pop out and let him know everything's all good. Let him know he doesn't have to pay double," Romero said.

"All right, so when do we start?" asked Sandra, coming off the bed.

"He should be here any minute, so…" Romero looked at his watch, informing them. Just then a knocking came to the door in the other room. Sandra, Jennybell, and Romero went to their places. Juliet closed the door between the rooms and went to sit down. She pulled a Snickers bar from her purse and silenced her hunger.

Sandra was the one to open the door. She greeted Mr. Marlongo with a bright smile and invited him to come in.

"Oh-uh, I was told Sweet Baby would service me," he said, looking surprised.

"She couldn't be here tonight, sorry, but me and my girlfriend here will be filling in for her. Can you handle two gorgeous women at the same time?" she said to him seductively. Jennybell waved from the bed and winked at him.

Mr. Marlongo was lost. This was not in the plan. Now that the original girl wasn't there, what was he to do now? God! He wished his luck wasn't so bad. If this wasn't a sting operation, he'd be about to stick it to two

125

chicks at the same time. Terry wasn't along though. He had help from the small transmitter in his ear in which the squad team across the hall could give him direction. The low male voice came in clearly.

"Marlongo, we are still a-go… Continue on as regular."

Terry understood and nervously finally answered, "Well it looks like I'm in luck." He smiled. "Let's do this."

Sandra smiled and came further into the room and sat down on the bed with Jennybell. "You know how this works, Mr. Marlongo. Show us your goods so we'll know everything is fine," Sandra told him.

The voice came over his ear receiver telling him to try and get around that part because it was called entrapment. They needed to hear the girl say they were selling sex for money.

"Come on, ladies. Let's all get naked and do this thing. I'm a repeat customer here."

"Ah-ah-ahh… house rules don't break. Show the dicky or no sticky," Sandra told him playfully.

He sighed. "All right, but I only brought eight hundred dollars. Me and Sweet Baby had a deal we worked out from time to time. Now, since it's two of you, does the sex cost double?"

A voice came over his earpiece saying, "Bingo, great."

"Before tonight you would, but right now… no, you get the two-for-one special," Sandra informed him.

Just then Romero emerged out of the bathroom before his cue. Mr. Marlongo watched him with unease as he came around the bed. "Mr. Marlongo, you've been playing games," Romero started sternly saying to him. "You know how this shit goes and yet you ain't did what was asked of you and you're asking dumb-ass questions. Tonight you're revoked, and 'm gon' have to ask you to leave."

Sandra and Jennybell were shocked but went with the program. They had no personal objections to the decision he was making. Mr. Marlongo was spooked and took a defensive step backwards, and in his earpiece he heard, "Go!"

Moments later the room door burst open and a group of law enforcement officers swarmed in with weapons ready. They shouted commands and orders for the people inside to "Get down! Get down!"

Romero flinched with his street instinct telling him to run, but as soon as he took fleeing steps nowhere he was bum rushed to the ground hard. Sandra and Jennybell shrieked and balled up on the bed in frightful caution. They too were rushed and apprehended.

Next door Juliet's heart was racing like a horse and pounding like a drum. She heard the commotion and jumped up and listened at the door. She could hear shouting and crying. It was the police, the police had raided. Juliet was beyond scared. She had to get out, she had to escape from the hotel or they would all be in jail. So she frantically started running around the suite gathering up important things such as purses and keys.

When she had everything, she went to the door and slowly opened it a little. She couldn't see anything but the room doors across the way, but she could still hear the commotion. So she opened the door a little bit wider and saw only other room-holders peeking their heads out of their doors. Behind Juliet, the door handle on the connecting door rattled and that was all the push she needed to dash out of the room and down the short hall where she rounded the corner to the B section. She saw the elevator ahead and sprinted to it. When she was there, she pushed the buttons wild and blindly until the doors opened. Juliet rode the elevator down to the lobby and got off clutching the three purses to her chest. She did her best to act natural but she found herself speed-walking with tunnel vision for the front exit. When she stepped foot on the parking lot, she jogged with haste to the car and jumped in. Juliet wasn't the best driver but she drove herself away from the hotel. She drove away sobbing and screaming obscenely.

 * *   *

It was a Monday morning. The sun was shining and the domestic birds were chirping. South Beach thrived with beachgoers. Shop owner, tourism, and family living. All seemed well, if you stood on the hillside looking down at the wonderful city, but a lot of it was cosmetic because it was what you didn't know… people were suffering.

When Juliet woke up she was all alone. She lay in the middle of her bed curled up like a small kitten. Her eyes were crusted over in their corners with dried out tears. At first she didn't understand why she was alone, or why the apartment was deathly quiet, but then she remembered. Coming into the living room, she tiptoed like she was trespassing. She was lost. She really didn't know what to do. She was once again alone. The only thing she could think to do was call Mama Ree back in Chicago and alert her to what was going on. Who else could she enlist help from?

"Girl, y'all out of control out there," Mama Ree said over the phone. "My son a grown man now and he controls his own thing, his own actions. But this is what you need to do. Call the county jail and ask what his bond is. Call me back when you find out."

When the call ended, Juliet called the county jail by way of phonebook and was told that Romero's bond was set at one million dollars. He needed ten percent of that to bail out. He was charged with accessory to murder, fleeing and alluding, white slavery, and intimidation to an informant. Sandra and Jennybell were charged with simple prostitution. Their bonds were both ten thousand dollars, which meant only a grand each.

Juliet was crushed to hear about the harsh charges her loved ones faced, especially Romero. She was about to call Mama Ree back, but when she searched for her number, she received a call from Romero himself.

"Oh my God, baby... are you okay?" she asked, overwhelmed with mixed emotions of happiness and sadness.

"Hell nah, I ain't okay," he told her. "Go into the bedroom and hit my safe. The code is 22-12-12. Take out ten grand and bond out the girls.

"How you know what their bonds are?" she wondered.

"Cause we all up in holding together. Sandra and Jenny are on the other side but when I came out for my call I heard 'em shout out to me. Look, these people talkin' murder and some more shit. I need to get out and get a lawyer."

"Did they question you?" she asked.

"Tried to, but I told they asses: lawyer. But anyways, go get the money and bond the girls out. As a matter of fact, no... find somebody else to do it cause they said they lookin' for you as well for questioning—"

"Me?!" she cut in, shocked.

"Yeah, you. Look, do like I said but be careful. When y'all three back together, we gon' work out a plan, aight?"

"Okay, okay, but baby... who do I get to bond out the girls?" she asked, puzzled.

"Juliet, you my bitch, my ace... find somebody. Get us the fuck out of here," he told her.

"All right." She nodded. "I'll find somebody."

"Aight, 'mma call back collect later on. Stay by yo' phone at all times, feel me?" he said.

"All right, I love you Romero," she told him.

"I know you do. Hurry up," he said, hanging up.

Juliet jumped up and dashed to the bedroom closet. She had to go get her family. She just hoped she wasn't caught in the process.

Chapter 16

Juliet called one of her repeat clients and asked him for a favor which was to bond out her girlfriends. His name was Alex Dunn, and he was the youngest client she serviced at only nineteen years old. Alex had a trust fund account worth three point four million dollars that was set up by his grandfather before he died. He was by society's standards an ugly person. He was fat, freckle-faced, and redheaded. Thing was… he was sweet and really liked Juliet. So when she called to ask for the favor, he had no problems doing what she asked of him, and at 3:30 p.m., Sandra and Jennybell were free.

"Thank you, Alex, really," said Jennybell as she exited the car and got into the Chrysler 300.

"Yeah, thank you," added Juliet who sat in the passenger's seat of his car. She was slightly paranoid to drive to the county jail herself so she parked the car a few blocks away and rode with him.

"It's not a problem, happy to help anytime," he smiled.

"Well that's good to know, because I may need you to do it again because there's more crap going on," she told him.

"Like I said, happy to help. Call me and I'm there," he assured her. Juliet leaned over and gave him a thankful peck to the lips, then she got out and got into her own vehicle.

"Where to?" Sandra asked, starting the car.

"Wait a minute," Juliet halted first. "What did you guys tell the police?"

"There was nothing to tell," Jennybell stated.

"Right," added Sandra.

"They didn't question you guys about anything?" Juliet said to them curiously.

"We said we wanted lawyers. Romero told us to lawyer up," Jennybell told her.

"So they did try?" she asked.

"Yeah, but we ain't say a word. We just asked for a lawyer," Jennybell told her.

Juliet looked at Sandra.

"That's what I did too, just like Romey told me," she told Juliet.

There was an awkward pause between them, then finally Sandra broke the silence. "Where to?"

"Home, and wait for Rome to call us with instructions," she explained.

The three headed to their apartment.

*   *   *

When Romero finally called, he told Sandra to go to their bank and pull out one hundred grand. After that, they all needed to put their heads together and find him the best lawyer who had a good track record of fighting cases of a high-profile nature. Once they accomplished that, they needed to tell him to arrange a visit with him ASAP.

So that's what the girls did. Sandra retrieved the money and they all searched the phonebook and internet for lawyers until they found the right one. His name was Peter Blackside. He was a veteran when it came to high-profile cases and was known for lending crucial advice to the team who got O.J. Simpson off. Blackside wasn't cheap either; his retainer fee was twenty-five thousand dollars cash, then, if he took on the case, his team charged $175 an hour. Romero had managed to save almost three hundred thousand so he was all right for the moment. He simply needed to get out so he could stack more bread for the battle the court system would bring.

When everything was all said and finalized, Romero was released on bail. He and his new lawyer parted was in the county jail parking lot with plans to speak again soon. Sandra and Jennybell were the ones to pick him up because Juliet was still wanted for questioning. She sat back at the apartment anxiously waiting.

"Goddamn! It feel good to be out dat bitch!" Romero said happy, giving kisses to the cheeks of his queens. "How my girls doin'? Y'all good?"

"Shit's been wild, Romey. What we gonna do now?" Jennybell asked.

"I know, but don't trip, we gon' get through this shit. Y'all wit' me, right?"

"Yeah," both girls responded in unison.

"Aight, den we all good. The main thing is not to panic," he told them calmly.

"Rome," Sandra called while driving.

"Speak on it," he answered.

She continued, "Umm... Juliet told us about what happen, you know... with that judge," Sandra said.

Romero nodded with an exhale. "Listen, we didn't tell you two because I felt that it was the best thing. The less you two know the less you to know when and if it came to being questioned by the police. It was for your own protection."

Even though Sandra and Jennybell hated to be left out and uninformed, they understood why he did what he did. The police were very tricky and manipulative, so the less they knew the better.

"What about me and Jennybell's cases? I mean... Can we go to prison?" Sandra asked, worried.

"Hell nah, this both of y'all's first major offense. Worst-case scenario probably thirty or forty days in the county with some probation. 'mma talk to my lawyer about it though because y'all linked to one of my charges. Just be smooth, shit gon' work out," he assured them both.

They rode down 64th Street headed towards home in silence. It was almost six o'clock at night and the sun was almost down. The scent of mouth-watering barbecue hit their nostrils as they entered the urban part of their route.

"Mmm, that makes me hungry," Jennybell sniffed.

"Straight up. In fact... pull into that joint comin' up," Romero pointed.

"Where? Lil' Porky's?" Sandra asked.

"Yeah," he confirmed.

When the clean Chrysler 300 pulled into the parking lot of the urban restaurant, the lot was busy with black folks coming and going. It reminded Romero of his hood back in the city. Hood-rats dressed provocative, street niggas dressed flashy while staying armed with illegal drugs and semi-automatic weapons. Coming from the city where gangs originated, Romero could see that he was in Blood territory by the overwhelming color of red most of the people wore. He was glad he and his girls had on neutral blacks, browns, and whites.

"What can I getchu, playboy?" the hip, old-school man asked

Romero behind the register.

"Uhh… let me get… five barbecue brats, four fries, and… four Sprites," Romero ordered.

"Okay, that'll be $17.65."

Romero stepped to the side and allowed Sandra to pay.

"Playa-playa, I see ya boy—boy got 'em trained to pay!" the hip old-school man joked.

Romero smiled, shaking his head. He handed Romero his receipt.

"Be about six or seven minutes. Next!" Old School said.

Romero, Sandra, and Jennybell stepped back and waited on their order. As they waited, making small talk, Romero noticed a group of three people sitting in the corner. Two males, one muscle-bound and the other small and snakish looking. There was also a female who looked oddly familiar. She was the main one of three who kept staring and whispering to the men. Sandra and Jennybell didn't notice what he did, but once Romero spoke on it, they slowly, inconspicuously turned and saw for themselves.

"Oh shit!" Jennybell cursed low as she turned back.

"What?" asked Romero, curious.

"That's Cherry Pie," she told him and Sandra.

"Who the fuck is Cherry Pie?" Romero asked, confused.

"West-Coast Red's old main girl. She was with him that night at the restaurant, remember?"

"Okay, so… be coo', fuck her. We get out shit and ride out. Sandra, go out and start the car."

When she left, Romero and Jennybell stood ill at ease. They could see from the corner of their eyes that the female known as Cherry Pie had recognized them both and was relaying a message to the men to make them look. Just then, the trio got up, tossed away their trash and headed for the exit that Sandra went out of. When the trio was only feet in front of Romero and Jennybell, Cherry Pie made sure she spoke her mind.

"White bitch let me find out you and this bubblegum pimp had somethin' to do with Red's murder, you and his ass gon' feel it," she said with sass.

Jennybell said nothing and Romero frowned with a flinch. The muscle-bound thug noticed his facial expression and took offense.

"What up, blood? You ain't like what she said?" he stopped and said to Romero.

The trio stopped, and now Romero and Jennybell were basically cornered. Romero wanted to meet aggression with aggression, but he couldn't afford to get into an altercation. He had too much on his plate.

"Ain't no problem big homie, I don't want no smoke," he calmly told the guy.

Cherry Pie interjected, "Where the money you owed Red? Cause you sho'll ain't pay! That's how I know you and this honky had something to do wit' what happen cause he was goin' to collect from y'all that night!"

By then, the other patrons in the restaurant were starting to pay attention to what was going on. Cherry Pie was getting irate. Romero's "spider-sense" was tingling. He was like a cat in a corner.

"What about Red? I don't know shit! We made plans and he never showed so that was on him," Romero said, playing mind games.

"So you gon' play stupid, huh?" Nigga, please. Yo' ass was the one, yo' ass and this white bitch!" Cherry Pie accused.

"Hey-hey now," Old School called over from behind the counter. "Y'all need to move dat outside."

"That split-second distraction from the man behind the counter was the opening that Romero needed, because as soon as the two men turned, he launched his assault on them both. Romero threw a hard stiff jab to the left side throat of the muscle-bound Blood. The right jab instantly sent the man stumbling backwards where he fell, holding his neck and choking. Romero quickly followed up with a hard, wild, but efficient left jab and right jab follow-up that connected to the smaller man's face. The force behind Romero's combo made the man stumble clumsily until he fell and crushed into the bottom half of the order counter. The unexpected rumble shocked all the bystanders inside the restaurant and dispersed the small crowd around it. Romero turned to see two things. Jennybell running out the side door and Cherry Pie going for something in her purse. Romero didn't hesitate when he saw her going for whatever it was, and he rushed over to her and gave her a wild right hook to the side of her head. Cherry Pie fell wildly to the ground where the contents of her bag spilled out. Romero didn't stay a second longer after that, he just dashed out the side door and headed for his car.

"Back out, back out!" Romero shouted with a wave as he rounded the building. Jennybell had just got in and Sandra put the car in reverse. When the car backed up, Romero ran right next to the passenger's side door. He wasted no time with the door so he dived head first into the window.

"Go, go, go!" he ordered as he pulled the rest of his body inside. Sandra stomped the brakes, twirled the wheel while putting the gear in drive and smashed the gas. Just then, Cherry Pie and the smaller man emerged out of the side door of the restaurant with guns ready. They both started firing, sending bullets zipping at and into the car. Sandra screamed in terror as the back window shattered completely. The sound of bullets hitting the car was like kids throwing rocks as you rode down the street. Sandra stepped on the gas and recklessly drove out of the lot into oncoming traffic. When she did, she sideswiped a van and almost made it fishtail out of control. Sandra managed to regain control just enough not to drive into oncoming traffic and made a wild turn on a red light where they got away. The rear of the Chrysler's engine sounded like a racecar as they drove down Division Street. Everybody in the car was on high alert as they headed for complete safety.

"What the fuck, man?!" Romero yelled in anger, sitting upright. "Damn! Y'all all good?"

Sandra answered with a trembling "Yes," but when Romero asked and looked back between the seats at Jennybell, he had to take a double look.

"Oh fuck!" he exclaimed with wide eyes.

"What?!" asked Sandra.

Jennybell lay on the backseat with open eyes, the side of her head was wide open and thick blood and brain matter was on her face.

"Jenny!" he called but got no answer. "Jennybell!"

"What? What? What?!" cried Sandra with fright.

Romero said back correctly in his seat and put his hands to his face. Sandra was crying and asking him over and over what was the matter but he was in a fog. It was as if he was underwater and all sounds were muffled.

*   *   *

When Detective John Rola heard about the recent shooting and death of a young girl, he didn't think too much of it, but once he heard the names of the victims involved, he immediately asked if he could lead the investigation. When he got to the county hospital, he found Romero Hinton and his girlfriend Sandra McNeil in the waiting area. They were being watched a patrolman when Rola came up on them. Both looked saddened and distraught.

"Well isn't this an unpleasant surprise? Mr. Hinton, you're just a glutton for punishment," Rola said, patting the patrolman on the shoulder.

Romero looked up at him with a solemn look. He wasn't in the mood for the detective's bullshit.

"Can you tell me what happened exactly?" asked Rola.

"I told him already, and the other police," Romero said with irritation in his voice.

"Well now you can tell me," Rola smirked.

Romero huffed and sat back. "Man... I just bonded out the county jail and on my way to the crib, me and my friends stopped to get something to eat. Two niggas, well, two guys and a female came up on me and my two girlfriends making threats, so I reacted the best way I knew how and started swinging. We ran and that's when the people started shooting at us, and killed my friend."

"So you provoked it?" Rola said.

"What?" Romero winced. "No... did you hear what I just told you?"

"Well... had to be positive. You're free to go for now but after we and my team re-review the tape and compile more witness statements, you may need to come down to the station and give a formal statement and possibly identify the attackers in a lineup... if we find them. Until then, Mr. Hinton... don't leave town."

Romero and Sandra stood up. His phone had been vibrating for the past hour but he simply ignored it. He knew it was Juliet but he didn't want to have to explain what happened over the phone.

"What's gonna happen with my friend?" Romero asked Rola.

"Her family or next of kin will be located and informed of her untimely death. From there her body will remain in the county morgue until her family or next of kin makes arrangements to move her," Rola explained to him.

"All right... well, what about my car?" he inquired.

"Seized, pending the conclusion of this investigation," Rola told him. "A squad car can drop you if—"

"It's coo'," Romero cut in. "We'll manage."

Romero took Sandra by the hand and led her out of the waiting area and out of the hospital. When they stepped outside, it was completely dark. Romero's phone vibrated in his hand and he finally answered it.

"Hello," he answered.

"Jesus! Why haven't you been answering my calls? Where are you guys?" Juliet asked.

Romero covered up the mouthpiece and looked over to Sandra and told her to call them a cab. He then returned back to Juliet. "Baby, we ran into a problem," he began, but found it hard to finish.

"Probably like what?" Juliet asked, concerned.

"Uh…" he cleared his throat. "Umm… Jennybell… she, she was shot—"

"What?!"

"She got killed, baby," he told her.

Juliet couldn't believe what she had heard. She was in complete disbelief. She went silent for a moment before the tears started to fall, then she began to sob uncontrollably. Romero did his best to console her but he couldn't get a comforting word in edgewise. Sandra, who stood next to him, could hear Juliet over the phone and like a chain reaction, she too began to cry softly for her slain sister. Romero placed an arm around her and just as she embraced him, Detective Rola came out of the emergency room doors.

"Mr. Hinton, change of plans. Gonna need you downtown now."

Chapter 17

The thing about bad luck is when it rains it pours. When the detective told Romero he needed him to come down to the station, it was because they had one suspect in custody. His name was Jamel Washington and he was the muscle-bound Blood who was with Cherry Pie and the other guy. He had been picked up for questioning after a nosy neighbor saw the news and reported him to the police as someone of interest. Thing was, Jamel wasn't guilty of any crime, he was just wanted for questioning. Crazy thing was, he wanted to press charges on Romero for assault and battery. So once again, Romero was arrested and booked back into the county jail not twelve hours after his first release. His lawyer did the best he could to show the judge that he wasn't in the wrong completely, but since his first case was so high-profile and the judge knew Tomas Difano… he revoked his first bond and spitefully gave him a new bond of two million dollars. Romero only had enough to keep his lawyer working his case so he couldn't bond out. He was back stuck in the county jail.

*   *   *

When Sandra had returned back to the apartment the night before without Romero, Juliet thought she would die. Sandra fell into her arms and they both cried, and when they were done, Sandra told her everything that had happened.

The house that Romero built had come crashing down. Things were worse than ever and once again Juliet was lost. The night Sandra told her what all took place was like a movie nightmare that invaded her life. That night they both slept in the master bedroom together. The only comfort they found was in the familiar embrace of each other's arms.

The next morning when Juliet awoke, she found herself in bed alone. It was almost noon and she couldn't believe she slept in so late. There were no missed calls from anyone.

"Sandy," she called out. Her head was hurting still from all the bogus information that filled it. The bright afternoon sun didn't make things any better as its rays beamed in on her puffy face. "Sandra!" she called again.

There was no answer, only silence. When Juliet got up and staggered to the front room, there was no Sandra, so she looked into Jennybell's room and found no one, then came up with the same results when she looked in her room. Juliet looked through her phone and called Sandra. Moments later she heard a chime in the other room. When she went to see where it was coming from, she found the phone on the coffee table lying next to a note and a bank bag that had "First National" on it. Juliet took a seat and read the note.

It said:

Juliet, I'm sorry but I can't stay any longer. Everything has changed and I have as well. I went to the bank and closed out the account. In the bag is all the money that was left in the safety deposit box. I kept the twenty-nine hundred that was in the savings. I'm going to go visit Romero at the county jail to say my goodbyes face to face… he deserves to hear my reasons for leaving from me. Thank you for being such a dear friend and sister to me. I'll never forget you. I love you.

Sandra "Baby Girl" McNeil

P.S. I kept my ring. I'll never get rid of it.

Juliet was hurt behind the departing letter. Tears bubbled on the lids of her eyes and ripped down her reddened cheeks. Setting down the letter, she picked up the bank bag, unzipped it, and laid eyes on a thick pack of crispy one hundred dollars bills. Some people would be filled with glee to possess that much money, but the money only solidified the fact that things were at their worst… and she was utterly alone now. Alone and pregnant.

Juliet's stomach twisted and turned. She felt sick, and seconds later with a mouthful of unknown stomach contents, she vomited into the toilet. On her knees, she spit the last nasty tasting chunks into the bowl and fell to the side of the bathtub with closed eyes and heavy breathing. The room was spinning. Just then, she heard her phone ring in the living room. It had to be Romero, she thought. She scrambled to her feet and ran back into the living room and answered it.

"Hello! Hello!?" she said anxiously. The automated voice came over the other end and told her she was receiving a collect call from an inmate at Long Beach County Jail, and would she accept. She did without hesitation.

"Hello, Romey?" she asked.

"Yeah baby, it's me," he told her.

"God, it's so good to hear from you. What the hell, man?"

"I know. Shit fucked up right now. Sandra just came from seeing me. You know she left right?"

"Yeah, she left a note and your money. Baby, what's gonna happen now?" she asked.

"'mma need you to take care of the business. 'mma need you to boss-bitch up and follow directions," he told her.

"What can I do? Tell me."

"Look, it's like one-sixty in the bag, right?"

"Umm... I guess."

"Yeah, well, it should be. Look, pay the rent for the next six months, aight. Then cuff sixty rocks and hold it down. Give my lawyer the rest. He gon' come by the apartment and pick it up around two or three o'clock. After that, 'mma need you to shoot to the city. My cuzo Nuk know you comin' and Mama Ree do too. Look, Nuk gon' help you flip the sixty rocks so I can possibly bond out again. My cuzo already know what I want and need... I need a 'whole thang.' Do you understand?"

Juliet didn't but she understood that whatever he was talking about, he was speaking in code. He didn't want the police to know just in case they were listening in.

"Baby, I don't understand, but I understand," she told him.

Romero had to be clever. "Remember Vegas?" he asked.

"Yeah."

"Remember what Jennybell got punished for?"

"Uh-huh."

"Good, that's what I need done with the sixty, only I need you and Nuk to hustle. I need a 'whole thang.' Understand now?"

Juliet computed what he was saying and her best guess was she was to take the money to Chicago and get with his cousin. Then he was supposed to buy a kilo of drugs, heroin, which was what Jenny got caught shooting in Vegas. She and Nuk were to sell the drugs to make the money to get him out on another bond. Juliet believed she understood. "I understand, babe. What about you? I can't just leave you out here alone," she told him.

"Baby, you have to. I can't stay in here. My lawyer says he could possibly draw this case out for over a year. I can't be in here for no year. You got to boss-bitch up and take care of the business like I know you can. My cuzo gon' do his best to make sure you well. He gon' give you 'the game.' Just make sure you stay on top of everything and don't be afraid to ask him questions. Look, I love my cuzo, but he ain't you. You are my rock, my heart… and at the end of the day, ain't nobody got me like you."

Romero's words were filled with truth, knowledge, and inspiration. Juliet was scared of what was ahead of her, but she had to push through. She had to help free her man.

"You understand me, don't chu?" he asked her.

"Yes, Romey, I understand. You can count on me, baby," she assured him.

"I know it. Go 'head and start packin' yo' stuff. I'll call you later on or tomorrow, aight?"

"All right, but dang, hold on, can't we keep talking until the time runs out?" she asked, not wanting to hang up just yet.

"Yeah, we can keep talkin'," he told her. And that's what they did. They kept conversing until the time on the call concluded.

*   *   *

When Juliet arrived at O'Hare, she met Nuk at the west gate. She was dressed in an all black outfit; black blouse, black spandex leggings, and four-inch heels. Her short blonde hair was nicely done and her eyes were covered with a large black pair of Tom Ford sunglasses. She carried three items: her purse, and two suitcases. When Nuk saw her coming out of the terminal, he thought, "Damn! This bitch lookin' good."

"So what did Rome tell you?" Nuk asked. He drove his truck down the Eaton Expressway heading out west.

"He told me you would help me find a kilo of heroin, and that you would help me sell it so I can post his bail," she told him.

Nuk chuckled to himself, shaking his head.

"What?" Juliet said, curious. "That's what he told me."

"Right-right… um, just sayin'… shordy, a brick ain't easy to cop. It might be a few days before I find a mufucka wit' dat kind of work, then I got to find a mix-master to stretch the dope," he explained.

"Whatever it takes." She shrugged.

Nuk rolled his eyes. "You got the money on you?" he asked.

"I only have ten thousand on me. The rest is downtown at the post office on… uh… Congress and Franklin."

"Downtown? On Congress? Why is it at the post office?" he asked, confused.

"I overnight mailed it to myself. You can only travel with ten thousand in cash by plane."

"Oh yeah? So when do we pick it up?" he asked.

"First thing in the morning."

"Aight, cause 'mma be on the hunt, and if I find that 'mma need the bread."

"How much do you think you can get one for?" she asked.

"A brick? Uh… 'bout… fifty-five, sixty. Depends on the quality."

"Rome told me you were gon' put me up on game?"

"Yeah, 'mma school you to the do's and don'ts. 'mma set you up in a spot where you ain't gotta do nothin' but serve and collect, serve and collect," he told her.

"How much can you make off a kilo?"

"Depends. 'Bout 250 to 350 thousand, if the dope real good. If cuz need two hundred rocks to walk den 'mma make sure we make the brick do numbers," he assured her.

"How long will it take?" she continued to ask.

"Damn, shordy, you wired or some shit? You sho'll askin' a lot of questions," Nuk said, slightly irritated.

"Rome told me to ask questions."

"Yeah, but damn… be coo', 'mma let you know everything once we get to the spot," he told her.

Nuk drove to the Travel Lodge Motel out on the south side on 86th and Cottage Grove. He was going to swing by Mama Ree's house first but he wanted to get Juliet settled in first, letting her drop off her bags, shower, or whatever. Nuk also wanted to check out a few people he knew on his side of town about copping major work.

"Aight, shordy, this here is the spot—yo' spot. The lil' rent been paid for the next month, so don't trip off dat. This area is dangerous. Niggas out here selling dope and guns, but it's a free market so you ain't got to trip about stealin' other mufuckas' clienteles. Uh… yeah, this is the spot. I got a key and you gon' have a key, aight? 'mma spin off for a lil' bit to see what's what out

142

in the land. You chill out here for a few hours until I spin back. 'mma take you out west to Mama Ree's crib so y'all can get a understanding or whatever, aight?"

"All right," she said to him.

"Aight den, don't open this door for nobody," he warned. "Hit me on my jack if you need me."

"I will," she told him.

When Nuk went out, Juliet bolted the door and looked out of the window. The parking lot was half full and she could see up and down the main street of Cottage Grove. She took a quick tour of the small room and found it to be like any other motel room. She turned on the TV, sat on the single queen-sized bed, kicking off her heels, and relaxed. Not twenty minutes later, she was passed out napping for jet lag.

  * *   *

It was around 6:30 at night when Nuk dropped Juliet off at Mama Ree's house. she had fixed a meal just for them that consisted of fried chicken, Velveeta cheese and shells, and sautéed spinach. Even though Juliet had spent time with Mama Ree the year previous, it hadn't been as intimate as this. Mama Ree was comfortable but Juliet was a bit nervous.

"Girl, how in the hell did my son get so caught up? They talkin' murder and white slavery and all this junk," Mama Ree asked.

"Mama Ree, I don't know... but he gon' beat those charges," Juliet answered, coy.

"Lord have mercy, y'all out there... doin' God knows what! Now y'all all messed up. Romero told me the other girl got shot and killed... Woo! Lord y'all need to pray, child."

Juliet wanted to cover her ears when it came to hearing anything about Jennybell. It was still a subject she still hadn't fully faced as of yet.

"I know, Mama, I know," Juliet could only say.

"So you gon' sleep here tonight."

"Mhmm," Juliet said with chicken in her mouth. "Mmm... just until Willie come and pick me up in the morning."

"Since you way out here and my son way out there, he sent you to take care of some business."

"Yes, ma'am."

"Business with my nephew, Nuk?"

"Mhmm," she nodded.

Mama Ree gave her a look that said "You must be crazy."

"What? Why do you look like that?" asked Juliet, curious.

"Girl, look. Willie is my sister's son, my blood… but he can be trouble. I just hope you know what you're getting into, cause if you doing whatever business with him… I know it ain't safe, and I know it ain't legal."

Juliet listened to the wise words of Mama Ree. She knew from the stories Romero told her that his cousin was dangerous, but he also told her that he was completely loyal to him and would never betray their bond. "I can handle myself, Mama," she assured her.

"Okay," Mama Ree said, nodding. "I hear you."

That night, Juliet borrowed Romero's old room which was now converted into a place that stored random items. Mama Ree had cleared it out enough to where Juliet could envision how Romero lived before she knew him. She looked at framed photos that hung on the walls, photos of a much younger Romero. He was so small and happy looking, she thought. There were also badges of merit for writing programs and contests. Juliet became sad looking at her beloved man and started to cry a bit. She missed him. She missed Sandra and Jenny. She missed her family… her kingdom.

A startling knock came to the door and as Mama Ree entered, Juliet wiped away her tears, pulling herself together.

"Baby, I—" Mama Ree began to say, but halted. "Girl, what's the matter?"

Juliet shook her head, doing her best not to continue crying, but tears escaped her eyes.

"Oh child, c'mere," Mama Ree said, holding out her arms.

Juliet came over and was enveloped by her warm embrace. It was there that she fully released her heavy heart. Like a mother holding a weeping child, Mama Ree rubbed Juliet's back while comfortably cooing her to calm herself. Mama Ree understood all too well why the young girl was so woeful. It was because, just like Mama Ree with Romero's father… she missed her man.

"Come on," she told Juliet, taking her by the shoulders. "Come on, you all right, you just goin' through it."

Juliet stood before her, pulling herself together. She was embarrassed and giggled uncomfortably, wiping her face clear.

"Here, I came to give you this." Mama Ree took her hand and placed a silver .22 revolver in it. Juliet was shocked and confused, and before she could protest, Mama Ree gave her an explanation. "You need to have protection out here, because it's a jungle full of animals. This is my gun, it's clean, never been used. Take it, and if you can, return it back to me when your business is done here."

Mama Ree smiled and simply left out of the room, saying, "Goodnight."

Juliet stood there looking down at the gun with its polished wooden handle. She could see bullets loaded in the rotary chamber. She placed it carefully into her purse.

Chapter 18

After eating a hearty homemade breakfast, Nuk came and picked Juliet up. They drove downtown to the post office and she picked up her package. Nuk told her that he had successfully found a cop man who would part with a brick of H. The cop man, in fact, were two brothers by the names of Big Twin and Lil' Twin. They lived on the Southside down on 73rd and Southshore Drive. The twins were big time drug lords; their names rung bell throughout the city and they were not to be trifled with. Nuk was supposed to call one of the twins' underbosses to set up a meet once he was ready to purchase. They were to meet in the Southside projects on the lower end called "The Ickies."

Before Nuk did any of that, he went back to the motel with Juliet and made sure all the money was accounted for. The twins didn't want a penny less than fifty-five thousand.

"Aight. Ten, twenty, thirty, forty, fifty!" Nuk counted carefully. He had placed five groups of ten thousand dollar bundles next to him on the bed. "And five. Done."

Nuk gathered up all the buy money, placed it in a small brown paper bag, and put the rest of the extra money back into its bank bag.

"Aight shordy, I'll be back in about two hours," he told her as he stood and tucked the rolled up bag down his pants.

"Whoa, hold on. I'm going with you," Juliet told him, coming off the dresser.

"Hell nah, shordy," Nuk halted. "You can't ride."

"Forget that, man, that's over fifty grand you got stuffed down your pants and you're not gonna just leave with it without me!"

"Shordy, 'mma come back in two hours. Chill."

"I'm going. Let's go," she said, heading for the door.

Nuk grabbed her arm and Juliet wrenched away. "Don't!" she warned.

"Fuck you meant 'don't'? You ain't comin', period! You a fuckin' honky! These niggas ain't playin' no games! If they see yo' white ass wit' me,

146

they ain't gon' do business and they might even wanna kill me! You ain't comin'! Just chill the fuck out and 'mma be back in like two hours."

Juliet wished she was stronger; a man, even. She knew she couldn't go but she tried her best to assert herself. She would just have to trust him. Nuk, on the other hand, was ready to smack the spit from her mouth. He hated to argue, especially with females… but, he respected his cousin too much to lay hands on his chick.

"All right… go, but you better be back here in two hours, Willie."

Nuk smirked and shook his head. He then left out of the room, letting her know "two hours."

When Nuk met up with the dope-man, the transaction went down smoothly. After that, he called and picked up Charlie Brown who was a dope-fiend and mix-master. When they made it to murder town where Nuk lived, it was straight to work. Heroin was a sensitive drug, Nuk knew. It was a living organism that could be stretched if you mixed it just right with the right amount of ingredients. Thing was, he wasn't good at mixing; he was a seller, and sometimes a stick-up kid. That's why he enlisted Charlie Brown, because he was a user who had been doing and mixing drugs for over thirty-two years.

"Tell me what ya need, tell me what you want," Charlie Brown said to Nuk. He sat at the kitchen table with all the equipment he needed to get started.

Nuk took a seat across from him to watch him work. He still didn't trust him.

"I need two ounces whipped. Thirty… no, twenty-two grams of mix on each one. Thirty Dome pills and seven grams of Baseo foil clips. Dimes and dubs only. Then mix up another two but keep 'em whole. Just foil 'em whole, aight?"

"Three ounces. Two in bags and one full?" he asked, guessing.

"Four ounces, man. Two in the foils, dimes and dubs, and two full ounces unfoiled," he told him clearly.

"Bet, I gotchu. Now, how much you breakin' me off wit'?" Charlie Brown added.

"'mma hit chu wit four grams," Nuk told him.

"Unmixed, right?"

"Yeah, unmixed. Let's roll man cause I gotta be somewhere in an hour and a half," Nuk told him impatiently.

And that's what Charlie Brown did. For the next hour he mixed, weighed, and placed the dope in folded squares of tinfoil. Nuk on the other hand worked his salesman skills over his cell phone. He called up every street nigga that was in his phone that bought and sold dope. He also told those same people to inform any snorters they knew that he had free dope samples. Nuk also called up his small clientele and informed them of the same thing.

Once the dope was mixed and Charlie Brown was paid, Nuk headed back over to the motel. He was on high alert when he parked because he knew all too well how easy it was to get stuck-up, and since he was holding over a kilo of mixed heroin… it was a stick-up kid's biggest dream. So before he exited his truck, he made sure he had his trusty TEC-9 tucked and ready.

When he came into the room, he found Juliet sitting on the bed with the TV off.

"How'd it go?" she asked calmly.

"Straight," Nuk said, going over to the bed and sitting his backpack on it. He then pulled out the dope that was mixed and bagged, and the rest of the key that was inside a large mason jar. Juliet examined the dope with strange looks. She had never seen drugs such as that.

"Look, shordy, tune in cause I can't be constantly repeating myself. There are thirty-six ounces in a key. I took four ounces and added mix to two and two. Two ounces got packaged up in tens and twenties. Those are for hype sales. The other two will be for you. You gon' keep the whole key but you gon' only sell them two ounces for now. 'mma ride out and see some people and I might run into some guys who want weight, so 'mma send the guys over here and all you got to do is call me to confirm the buyer and make the sale. Look… listen now, here come some numbers. Each ounce sold in 'bags,' foils, gon' bring in anywhere from $5,500 to $6,000. Each full ounce sold gon' bring in $2,500. Now, if we 'jook,' meaning work hard… we can make that $200,000 for cuzo."

Juliet nodded, she was ready to get started. "How much do you think we can make all together?" she asked.

"Depends… with all the shorts? At the least… 260 to 325 thousand," he told her.

Juliet was blown away. She didn't know the drug game was so

lucrative. She smiled a bit.

"Look, 'mma stash this jar under the bed in between the springs so don't be jumpin' on the bed and shit," he said.

"Why would I be jumping on the bed?" she asked, puzzled.

"'m just sayin', don't be rough. Keep these two ounces in the bottom dresser drawer, put some socks and panties over them or some shit. This motel room finna be yo' home for at least the next two to three months, but… This land ain't yo' home, it's mines. Chitown is a beast that will chew yo' ass up and fuck spit you out… it'll eat you up. Follow my lead, sit back and collect this money. You ain't here to make friends or go shoppin' at the malls… you here for one reason and that's money. You ain't no prisoner but this ain't no open spot where you can be all outside just strollin' around. Stay low key. You don't know these niggas out here and you don't need to know these niggas out here. You need to get out for a while, go to the store for something, call me. I come take you or bring whatever to you. Aight?"

"All right," Juliet nodded.

Nuk got down on the floor and stashed the mason jar full of dope inside the box spring. Moments later, his cell rang and he answered it. "What it do?" he answered, standing up. "Give me twenty minutes."

When he hung up, he gathered the two ounces of dope he had bagged up and stashed them down his pants. Juliet noticed he had some type of weapon tucked in his waistband.

"What's up?" she asked, curious about his call.

"That was money right there. Time to go make it happen."

*   *   *

When the ball began to roll on Operation Free Romero, it rolled hard and extremely well. Nuk never had a problem with selling dope; it just wasn't his primary source of income. But now that he was armed with more than his usual fourteen grams, he thought seriously about making the dope game his one and only. Nuk sold dope from the south side of town to the west side. His phone was constantly bombarded with calls from clientele wanting his dope. The money was coming in fast. He would make over $100 an hour on average and over $180 to $200 on an above-average hour. Juliet was also following instructions. Just like Nuk said, he would send over a few guys he dealt with every two or three days. The guys would come and knock, she would ask their names, call up Nuk to confirm the sale, retrieve the dope, and collect the money. Juliet found out that she didn't care about being cooped up in her room. She just stuck to a schedule that kept her entertained. Nuk made sure that work hours went from six a.m. to 9 p.m. only. In between that time, Juliet would spend her time pigging out on fast food and pizza deliveries. She would also speak on her cell with Romero twice each day and they would talk about life, the coming baby, and the future. Some days, Mama Ree would ask Romero about Juliet when he called and the next day Nuk would come pick her up and take her out west to spend the entire day. Mama Ree was overly excited when she was finally told she would become a grandmother soon. She took it upon herself to start looking and pondering baby names. Romero and Juliet had already decided to name the baby after him if it was a boy, and name the baby Eastern Star Hinton if it were a girl.

By the end of the first three weeks, there was already over forty-eight thousand dollars made towards the Free Romero fund, and Nuk expected to do twice that much over the coming three weeks.

Back in Long Beach, Romero's lawyer was going over his case with a fine-toothed comb. He somehow managed to get the charges of white slavery and intimidation of an informant dropped, but still couldn't land a bond reduction. The state's attorney's office smelled blood and wanted Romero. They were building a solid case that was packed wall to wall with circumstantial evidence.

Through the lawyer-client privilege, Romero told his attorney, Alex Blackside, everything he wanted to know, and in doing so he had a better view of how to attack key issues. Mr. Blackside was even pushing for a plea of not guilty and wanted the case completely thrown out on the grounds that the state was on a witch hunt and wanted to burn the first person who fit their weak criteria. The state simply returned with a plea bargain of five to fifteen years. Of course, Mr. Blackside quickly turned them down and told them to prepare for trial. In doing so, the state beefed up the charges from accessory to first-degree murder. Now he faced time ranging from twenty-five years to life. It was devastating news, but Mr. Blackside assured Romero that it was a smokescreen. Just a scare tactic to get him to plea out.

When Romero called and told Juliet, she simply started crying from heartbreak, but he assured her just as his lawyer assured him that it was all a play. So as time went on, Nuk and Juliet did their best each day to sell their product. Juliet's stomach began to stick out a little bit and she could really begin to feel motherly. Every so often, she would send Romero one or two hundred dollars through Western Union so he could have funds on his books for commissary.

*   *   *

As warm water and scented soap rinsed down Juliet's body, she heard the front door of her motel room open.

"Willie?!" she called out.

"Yo, yo!" he answered her.

"Did you bring me food?!"

"Popeye's!" he told her.

Juliet stepped out of the shower, dried herself off, slipped on panties and wrapped herself with the towel. When she came out, she found Nuk sitting with his shoes off at the small table. He was counting wads of cash.

"What's up?" she said, grabbing the bag of food off the dresser and taking it to the bed.

"Shit... tired, ready to lay up wit' a skeezer," he told her.

"Did you do good out there?"

"Sixty-five hundred... where dat money you made today?"

As Juliet munched on Cajun fries, she leaned over, retrieved a folded wad of cash and tossed it over to him. Nuk caught the money and just as he did, something else caught his eye... Juliet's panty-covered crotch. Nuk saw that she wasn't conscience of her legs being so wide open, and he seized the opportunity to sit in a position where he could see without being noticeable.

As she ate, he counted money and watched, watched and started to lust with thoughts of having sex with her.

"How much is there?" she said with a full mouth, turning the TV.

"'Bout nine rocks. We got almost a hundred rocks."

"Mm... good, Romey gon' be happy to hear that."

"Did you call his lawyer?"

"Nope, but he called, Rome did. He supposed to call again soon."

"Oh yeah... aight," Nuk said, getting up. He went over to the closet area and pulled up the heating vent from the floor. From inside, he pulled out a paper bag which held all the rest of the money. He then put the nine thousand inside and put the bag back where he got it. Nuk tossed a loose shirt of Juliet's over the vent for good measure. Rounding the corner, Nuk

151

found himself horny and semi-hard. He wanted to fuck Juliet and was about to see how he was gonna do it. So he came and sat right behind her at the top of the bed. Juliet simply scooted forward a little, continuing to eat and watch TV. Nuk looked at her short wet hair and let his eyes slowly look at her soft neck and bare shoulders.

"Can I ask you a personal question, shordy?" Nuk said.

"Mhmm," she said, nodding but not turning. She was too busy eating.

"Nuk asked, "You got a bra on under this towel?"

"Uh-uh, why you ask?" she said, still not turning.

Nuk didn't answer her, he just reached over and from behind grabbed her left breast. Juliet was shocked but didn't react. She just looked down at his hand and told him, "Willie... don't do that."

But he kept squeezing. "'m sayin', shordy... let a nigga fuck somethin'."

Juliet calmly pushed his hand away and turned around to face him, but once again she sat with one leg up on the bed and her crotch was exposed. Nuk noticed from the corner of his eye.

"Willie, you know 'm wit' yo' cousin and 'm pregnant with his baby... You wrong," she told him lightly.

"'m just sayin'... pussy lookin' real fat right now," he said slowly, looking down.

Juliet smacked her lips and closed her legs. "Boy... you need to quit," she said, rolling her eyes.

"Quit? Man, shordy, my joint rock hard and ready. All you godda do is put them panties to the side and let me slide in."

"Willie," she sighed. "Everything been going good. We makin' money, we been chillin'... don't ruin what we got goin'. You can go mess with any other female in Chicago and you wanna mess with your cousin's soon-to-be baby-mama. That ain't right."

Nuk made a "psss" sound, shaking his head in dismay. He knew she was right but he had to shoot one more shot.

"So a nigga can't even suck some pussy?" he asked.

Juliet got chills when he said that. She wanted to get some head— hell, she wanted to fuck. But her love for Romero wouldn't let her be disloyal.

"No Willie… not that either." She smiled a bit.

"Damn, aight… 'mma head out." He got up and prepared to leave.

Chapter 19

"Look, I godda spin outta town to Champaign-Urbana and make dese sales. 'mma be gone till the morning. I ain't got no people comin' over there so don't expect nobody," Nuk told Juliet while he drove.

"What about food?"

"Order some shit, or do you want me to swing back and take you to my auntie's house for the night?"

"Naaah, I'll be fine. Good money down in that place you going?" she asked, wondering.

"Sweet! Major bread down there. You gon' see, come back wit' like… ten or eleven rocks."

"Mm, well, good luck and please be careful."

"You know me. You be safe though, and don't open the door for no nigga," he warned her.

"I won't. Oh yeah, what about the rent? It's the ninth," she reminded him.

"Fuck! You wanna run it down there for me? 'm already on the e-way."

"Yeah, sure. How much is it?"

"$1,350," he told her.

"Wow… all right, I'll run it down in a little while."

"Aight, 'mma holla back. Till tomorrow, shordy," he told her before hanging up.

It was ten-thirty in the morning when Nuk called and right after that, Juliet went back to sleep. When she awoke around two in the afternoon, she was starving and decided to order herself pizza from Domino's. While she waited, she took all the money she needed to pay the room rent and the food bill. Stepping outside onto the top-level platform, Juliet took her first deep breath of fresh air in two days. The change in light made her eyes tingle and squint. She was dressed simple, in a powder-blue tank-top with blue jean shorts and a pair of female Nike Airmax. Juliet went downstairs and around the front to the front office. When she went inside, she stood behind a single customer. He was a young black guy whose pants sagged low off his rear-end. The young man turned and glanced at her and gave her a head nod saying "What hap'nin'?" Juliet said nothing, she just smiled in acknowledgement. Minutes later when the young black customer left and Juliet stepped up, she proceeded to pay for the rent. When she was through, she headed back to her room. As she rounded the corner and down the motel walkway there was a nice old-school Chevy parked in the lot. Juliet had to walk right in front of the car because it was parked at the curb. There were men inside the car and another on the outside bent down speaking to the driver through his window.

"What up, lil' mama?" the man said to Juliet as she passed. Once again she simply smiled without words. She just kept going until she reached the stairs and proceeded onward.

"White girl holdin' on the ass side," G-Moe said behind the wheel.

"On my mama, Moe. She super decent too," Lil' Moe added. There were three men watching her as she went about her business and entered into her room. The third man was in the back seat and his name was B-down. He was a rough drug addict who lived at the motel as well. The three men were conducting a little business. G-Moe and Lil' Moe were homeboys who had grown up together They were gangbanging thugs who didn't care about the true productivity of a law-abiding citizen. G-Moe, who was the oldest at twenty-two years old, stood 5'9", weighed 189 pounds, and was light skinned. Lil' Moe was younger at nineteen years old, standing 5'11", weighting 179 pounds, and was slightly darker than his buddy.

The reason for the two hoodlums' presence at the motel was because of their number-one client, B-down. B-down had strong-arm robbed a "Chinaman" for his weekly take of cash from his store as the man took it to his bank. Now, B-down was spending the entire eleven thousand dollars on heroin with them. B-down had been staying in the motel room snorting his life away for three straight days. He had bought some individual blow bags from another drug dealer because he couldn't find G-Moe and Lil' Moe, but once he ran out, he went and found his suppliers.

When the good-looking white girl had entered her room, the three men in the lot continued.

"I think dat der white hoe might be selling something'," B-down told them as he dipped his pinky finger into a small plastic bag corner and tasted the dope.

"Say what? Sellin' what?" asked G-Moe, turning his head to see B-down in his peripheral view.

"Gotta be somethin', G-Moe, cause since I done been down here, I done seen plenty a' niggas come and go from up there, and these the street niggas. Look like the folks from down on 67th or 68th.

"Get the fuck outta here," Lil' Moe said to him in disbelief.

"On my dead mama soul, Lil' Moe, I ain't gon' lie. Two, three times a day sometimes, niggas be up there, and it be in and out, quick, boom! Like they had called ahead of time and the white bitch was waitin'. Right hand to God."

Lil' Moe and G-Moe looked at each other. They didn't like to hear that some unknown person was in their area selling and/or getting money without their consent. This was a no-no in Chicago and for somebody to do it like it wasn't nothing… meant they were either from outta town or just stupidly bold. But G-Moe and Lil' Moe thought alike; they were both thinking kick-door robbery time.

"Who else be up there? The white bitch can't be on her own. I can't see that," G-Moe asked.

"Some nigga in a truck, folks lookin' nigga. He shoot through all the time and be up there the longest. He got a room key in fact," B-down reported.

"Mm, oh yeah. You ain't never seen none of these studs around?" G-Moe asked.

"Not me, uh-uh."

"Lil' Moe interjected; he had just remembered something. "On my mama, G-Moe… the bitch was just inside wit' me, and when I turned around, she had a big ass rack in her hand."

"That's because she probably payin' rent. You know you can rent for up to a month at a time," B-down chimed in.

"Mhmm, had to be at least a stack or better… yeah, mufucka workin' up there," Lil' Moe said, turning to look up at the room door. G-Moe had heard enough, he was now formulating a plan, but he couldn't speak around B-down.

"Aight, B-down, we'll holla atcha in a minute."

"Damn, y'all just gon' kick a nigga out, huh? G-Moe I'll kill yo' phony ass," B-down joked as he collected his things to exit. Lil' Moe got back into the passenger seat next to his partner. They watched as the hyper drug-head speed-walked back into his room.

"What up? Cause I know we in that bitch," Lil' Moe said. He was speaking about the white girl's room.

"Hell yeah we in that bitch. We just gotta chill and watch dat bitch for a while, see what we see first," G-Moe told him. Just then they saw a pizza delivery car from Domino's enter the lot and drive slowly behind them. They watched as the car parked, a man got out with his pizza case, dashed up the stairs, and knocked on a customer's door.

"Buddy probably goin' to ol' girl room," G-Moe said as he watched. "Yup… there she go."

The pizza man had indeed delivered to the white girl, and once the pizza man was paid and on his way out the lot, the white girl emerged from the room with an ice bucked and rounded the corner heading towards the ice machine. A few minutes later, she rounded the corner and reentered her room.

"Come on," G-Moe said, starting his car. "Let's go gear up and swing back later on."

"Should we call B-down and tell him to call us if he see some more niggas come through?" Lil' Moe asked.

"Yeah, do dat."

*   *   *

Juliet had spent her day eating pizza, watching a "Bad Girls Club: Mexico" marathon, talking on the phone to Mama Ree as well as Romero, and sleeping. When she awoke this time, it was well after seven and dark outside. Once again she and the baby were hungry and so she ordered from Domino's again. This time she made it a large. While she waited, she took a twenty-minute shower. When she was done, she simply slipped on one of Romero's t-shirts and it was so large compared to her that it drooped off one shoulder and hung down to her shins. She watched "Hardcore Pawn" on TruTV for a while until the pizza man arrived. After she paid, she stole a quick slice and bit into it just before she scurried out of the room barefoot with the empty ice bucket under her arm. When she was done and had rounded the corner back to her room, she noticed two men down the walkway. They were both dressed in dark clothes and were turned seemingly in talks with one another. Juliet couldn't see their faces because it was dark in the section they were standing in, plus she really paid them no mind because she was already at her door and the men were halfway down.

When she placed the keycard into the lock, she entered into the room and like always she allowed the door to close behind her as she put the ice bucket down on the dresser.

As the door glided closed, an unexpected burst of sound made Juliet flinch wildly and shriek with a "Woo!" The two men from the walkway had bum rushed into her room with guns out. One of the taller men rushed over to her and grabbed her by the neck hard. He put his large gun close to her face. Juliet's face was distorted with pain and fright overtook her. She managed only broken words in protest. "Ah! No, plea—heell," she groaned.

"Bitch you better shut the fuck up or 'mma shoot the shit out of you!" the man hissed at her. With that warning being said, Juliet went rigid with her mouth ajar with terror. The other man closed and locked the door before turning into the room with his gun drawn.

"Who else in dis mufucka?!" the shorter man aggressively asked.

"Nobody," Juliet cried softly.

The man closed the door then moved quickly and cautiously over to the bathroom. As he went to search, the other darkly cloaked man looked around the room.

"Clear, G-Moe?" the man asked with a racing heart. The shorter man, better known as G-Moe, came out of the bathroom with his gun raised and aimed it at Juliet's face. She flinched with closed eyes. The man wore a snow mask.

"Aight, bitch! Where the shit at?" G-Moe said.

Juliet hesitated. She didn't know what to do. She couldn't tell the truth because if she did, Romero would be stuck. So she lied the best way she could. "Please! What stuff? I don't have anything."

"So you think this shit a game, huh?" G-Moe told her. He then hit her hard on the top of her head with the tip of his gun. Juliet cried out with pain, but no blood was drawn. "Where the shit at?!" he asked again.

"I don't... I don't have anything, I have some money in my p-purse," she cried and held onto her story.

G-Moe looked and saw her purse on the nightstand, before he

searched it, he found thirty or so odd dollars sitting out and took it, then he proceed to search the purse.

"Okay, okay, bitch… now we talkin'," he said, finding over $600.

"Now where the rest at? Don't lie cause a mufucka already done told us what up," G-Moe said, turning back to her. But before Juliet could say anything, the man began to lift up the mattress on the bed, and when she saw that, she knew that he was going to flip the box spring and find the rest of the kilo. She had to think fast.

"Please don't kill me. I just sell pussy, that's all. My man sell dope and he out of town," she told them.

"So where the nigga be puttin' the shit when he be here?" G-Moe asked, dropped the mattress back down. Juliet was relieved, then she continued with her plan.

"In the bottom drawer of the dresser, but I think he took his stuff with him. Ouch!" she said as her neck was crushed. Juliet wished she could get to her gun that Mama Ree gave her. She wondered how the robber didn't see it when he searched her purse.

"Move, Lil' Moe. Take dat bitch over to the bed."

G-Moe sat his gun on the dresser top and started searching through all the drawers. Juliet was pushed violently onto the bed where she flopped onto her front side. Her long shirt flew up and her naked rear end was exposed as the other man known as Lil' Moe crouched over her with one knee on the bed and his gun stuck in the crevice in the back of her neck.

"There we go!" G-Moe said happily.

"What up, Moe?" asked Lil' Moe.

"About an ounce of dope, low."

"Fuck outta here."

"On Jeff, boy! That bitch was lying," G-Moe said. He stood up and put the drugs into his pants, then he grabbed his gun and was about to leave.

"Let's—" he began to say but stopped. He came over and looked down at Juliet's naked butt. "Damn."

"What up? You tryna run somethin'?" Lil' Moe asked. He was speaking about having sex with the girl.

"Hell yeah," G-Moe said, unbuttoning his pants with lust. "We finna fuck you bitch. Don't put up no fight cause I'll kill you quick. You sellin' pussy anyways."

Juliet was more frightened than ever. She was about to be raped, what could she do? Scream? Fight back? She'd be killed. She and the baby would be dead and Romero would be alone fighting life in the penitentiary. She had to shut down… and let them have her.

"Watch out, Lil' Moe," he said, coming over with his hard dick out. G-Moe pulled a gold-packaged condom out of his pocket and rolled it on.

"Moe, you ain't got no mo'?" Lil' Moe asked hopefully.

"Nah, G… that's all I had." G-Moe got on the bed, pushed her legs apart, and stuck his dick inside her. Juliet cried out in pain because she wasn't lubricated nor were her emotions in it. The robber-rapist mounted her in a push-up position and started forcefully pumping in and out of her unwilling vagina. Lil' Moe got up and went to the window and peeked out. All was still and peaceful outside. Juliet groaned with each pump and gripped the bed sheets. Not more than two minutes later was the first man finished and pulling himself out of her.

"Come on, G," G-Moe said as he stuffed himself back into his pants, condom and all. Juliet tried to pull her shirt down but was told not to move. She turned to look back at the man and when she did, she saw that he had a tattoo on his stomach. Juliet couldn't make out the words just then because her eyes were so watery.

"Fuck that shit, Moe, 'm coo' wit' out a Jimmy. Let's bounce," Lil' Moe told him.

G-Moe pushed him no further and pulled himself together to leave, but not before he placed a warning on the white girl. He leaned over to tell her, "Bitch," he said, pulling her collar around her neck, making her head rise and choke, "You call dem people, 'mma find you and kill you. Pack yo' shit and don't go sellin' shit else around here." He then gave her a parting right hook to the back-right side of her head with his gun. The hard blow made a *tink* sound as it knocked Juliet unconscious.

Chapter 20

It was almost seven in the morning when Nuk pulled into the lot back in Chicago. He made over ten thousand dollars and had orders for more. He was happy to report his good fortune to Juliet. Nuk exited his truck and headed upstairs. When he got to the door and opened it, he was frozen stiff when he saw what he saw. Nuk's heart began to speed up and his senses went on red alert. So he checked his surroundings before he pulled out his TEC-9. From the doorway, he could see Juliet laid face down on the bed. She was still half naked and still. Coming further into the room, he could see that all the dresser drawers had been pulled out; clothing was all over the carpet.

"Ah!" Nuk called to her. "Juliet!"

When she didn't move, Nuk came in more and from the corner of the dresser, assessed that the room was clear. Nuk then went to Juliet's side and saw blood in her hair. His first thought was she was dead from a bullet to the head. Pulling her shirt down, he carefully touched her back and shook her.

"Juliet," he called. "Juliet."

To his relief, she stirred and made an unknown audible sound. Nuk gently examined her head and saw that she only had a small gash. He really didn't know how to handle a situation like this, but he had enough brains to figure it out.

"Juliet… 'ay… shordy, wake up," he said to her lightly as he touched her back.

Drowsy and with an aching head, she began to wake.

"Shordy… what the fuck?" Nuk asked curiously.

"Hmmn… ah!" The tenderness of her head shocked her. Juliet opened her eye to see Nuk's dark face at her side. Then the memories of what took place while he was gone came flooding back. "They didn't get the money or the dope," she told him groggily while squinting. She turned over onto her side.

"What?"

"Two guys… they robbed us. They took the ounce from the dresser and some money from my purse… but that's it," she told him.

"How'd they get in? I told you to keep the door locked, shordy."

"I went to get ice because I had just ordered pizza. They rushed in."

"Nuk felt sorry for her and livid at the same time. He was also curious about the state and position she was in when he found her.

"Damn, shordy… you all right? I mean… when I came in, you were…" Nuk trailed off, hoping she would fill him in. She did.

"They raped me," she boldly said to him.

Nuk swallowed and flexed his jaw muscles.

"Fuck! Damn, shordy, I'm sorry… What you wanna do? Call them people?" he asked.

"No!" she objected. "We can't… I uh… we can't. I'll be okay, don't worry, but those guys said if we don't leave they'll be back and kill us."

"Us? They know me?" he asked, puzzled.

"No… I just said you were my boyfriend. They don't know who you are," she told him. Juliet stood up slowly and rubbed her belly. She was just glad she wasn't punched in the stomach or worse, killed. She touched the back of her head carefully and winced. She then moved to the front door, closed, and locked it. Nuk stuck his gun back into his pants. He watched as the little woman slowly made her way to the table where the pizza box was located. She opened it and removed a cold slice and took two hungry bites.

"Damn, shordy, you tough as hell," Nuk told her, getting up. "Go on 'head and sit down. 'mma gather all yo' shit and everything else. We finna get up out of here. Them niggas, did you recognize them or anything?"

Juliet chewed her food and nodded. She saw a pair of her clean panties on the floor and picked them up and put them on. Nuk saw her as he retrieved the cash from the closet floor. Juliet thought back but things were blurry.

"Uh… they seemed young, about eighteen to twenty-one. One was taller and the other slightly shorter. They kept saying 'Moe' or something."

Nuk came out of the closet, giving her his full attention. She had said some key words. "What? They said 'Moe'? Like what?" he asked.

"Uh… you know, like Moe this and Moe that… G-Moe—"

"G-Moe?!" Nuk cut in, roused up.

"Yeah. You know him?" she asked.

"If it's the same one. Did you see a black Chevy?"

"Black Chevy? Umm… oh! Yeah, when I came from paying the rent, there were some guys in the lot sitting in a black Chevy." Juliet could see it now. It was all so clear. It was the guys from the lot, the guy who was in front of her in the front office. Had to be.

"That bitch-ass nigga! 'mma kill that nigga. He probably had Lil' Moe or Rock'stone with—"

"Yeah, Lil' Moe!" she cut in. "Lil' Moe was the other guy's name."

"Psss… 'm finna murder them weak-ass niggas. See, them studs think they run shit. I know the niggas but we ain't buddies. They stay down on 83rd. I know where these dudes live and everything."

"But how would you get them?" she asked. "Not saying I want you to. I don't want you to get hurt or go to jail or anything."

"Man… them studs soft as fuck! See, I knew they brother—G-Moe brother—Will'kill, before he got killed back in 2000. Will'kill was a real standup nigga, but his brother and his lil' homies some hoes. They know me, and they sellin' 'harron' out G-Moe auntie crib."

Juliet took one last bite of her pizza and got up and carefully got dressed. Nuk watched her wince with pain as she pulled on her jeans. He was seeing red; he already knew he was going to pay the niggas back—tenfold!

"Cuz gon' flip out once he hear this shit."

"Please, let's just keep this between us. He… he doesn't have to know," she told him, pleading.

"Psss," Nuk sounded with a shaking head. "Aight shordy, aight. I ain't gon' say shit."

"Thank you. Where are we moving to?" she asked, helping him gather her things.

"'mma drop you off at the Robert's motel down on 64th. It's low-key," he told her.

"What are you gonna do? Because if it's to get those guys then I wanna help," she told him.

Nuk rolled his eyes like "Here we go," and Juliet noticed. She didn't care though. She wanted revenge, deserved it.

"Look, this ain't no game, we just can't roll up on these niggas together. Shit gotta be—"

"They raped me, Willie!" she cut in. "Do you know what that feels like? To be force-fucked by a stranger, huh? Don't take this away from me, please."

Nuk felt really bad for the girl and felt where she was coming from. Hell, he wasn't raped and he himself was for sure gonna get him some revenge. It was the disrespect that had him bloodthirsty. Out in his hood and many blocks surrounding it, he was known as a goon and a nigga not to be crossed. Nuk had killed before and it didn't faze his conscience, and he was fully prepared to kill again because he was built for that type of life. Nuk knew Juliet did indeed deserve some payback, and he wanted to help her get it. He just had to put his evil mind to work.

"Aight," he started. "Let me hit some blocks and go holla at my mans and them. 'mma hold you down but if I help you with this shit… you better not freeze or cur-up," he warned sternly.

"I won't. I promise I won't."

* * *

It was around noon when Nuk drove over to 65th and Normal to pay a visit to one of the richest street niggas he knew. The man's name was Sloppy and his name fit his look. Sloppy was an OG in the game. He made his fortune selling crack all throughout the 80s and 90s and now he just sat back like a fat rat and sold kilos of cocaine to half the Southside. Sloppy was black as night, 6'6" in height and 425 pounds of soft fat. Nuk used to sell coke for him a few years back and was his enforcer at times when guys came up short too many times on check-ins.

Nuk went his own way after awhile, but was still tight with the man. He needed him now because Sloppy had connections on guns and other related things. Nuk made sure he called ahead to get the okay to meet with him, and when he did, he headed straight over to his building.

"What's been up, young blood? Long time no see," Sloppy said.

Nuk sat across from the large man in his three-flat building. It was decked-out wall to wall with fine furnishing and large flat-screen TVs.

"Yeah, it's been a while," Nuk said.

"To what do I owe this visit? You said you really needed a favor over the phone."

"Yeah… um, I need to take care of some work and it requires that quite touch," Nuk said.

"That quiet touch, huh? You talking 'bout that extra piece for the

164

piece?"

"That's what 'm talkin' 'bout. Can you hold me down?" Nuk smiled.

"I can get you whatever you need, but you gots to come correct with that cheese," he told Nuk, simple and plain.

"I gotchu," Nuk said, patting his pocket.

"Aight. Let me call my white buddy."

*   *   *

When Nuk finally left Sloppy's, it was well after two p.m. Sloppy's "white buddy" arrived with three guns that were already equipped with blast suppressors. There was a .44 nickel-plated revolver, a .44 steel-plastic glock, and a small .380 semi-automatic. In the end, for eleven hundred dollars, Nuk bought the glock. From Sloppy's, he drove back to his house and left his car to jump on the CTA bus and journeyed out east. It was there that he found a steamer, which was a bogus low-key car, and stole it by way of hotwire. Nuk then drove back out south over to 83rd and Everheart where he knew G-Moe lived. Nuk had to be extremely careful with driving into unknown territory because the area he was in was known for gangbanging and "set-trippin'" on anyone they felt didn't belong in their hood. Luckily for Nuk, on this day there was little to no one out on the block G-Moe stayed on. When Nuk found the two-flat house, he pulled all the way into the driveway until his small Prius reached the garage located in the backyard. His heart was racing a million miles a minute but on the outside, he was calm, cool, and collected. Nuk loved the rush danger gave him. As he turned the car off and got out to go to the back door, he noticed someone peek out the house's backside window. Of course he showed no signs of noticing; he just continued to the door and knocked. There was low rap music coming from inside the house but once Nuk started to knock the music went off. Moments later, G-Moe himself opened the door.

"What the demo?" he asked down to Nuk with puzzlement. The white metal screen door was between them and Nuk stood calmly at the bottom of the short steps.

"What up, G-Moe? You remember me?"

"Yeah, you Nuk. You use to mess wit' my bro. What up?" he asked again.

"Mufucka just searched the land for some D and niggas dry. A nigga finna shoot out to Atlanta and I need some work. I remember Ill'will used to have shit on smash so I had to take my chances, feel me? 'm 'bout money."

G-Moe was fooled, and better yet he was attracted to Nuk's swagger, not to mention he was always up for making money. "Whatchu tryna get?" G-Moe asked.

Nuk looked around before he spoke and lowered his voice. "Mufucka need whatever five racks can get."

"Five racks?" G-Moe asked. He had heard him the first time; he just couldn't believe his luck.

"Step on in, bro," he told Nuk, unlocking the screen.

When Nuk stepped in, his nostrils were hit hard with the strong scent of kush weed. G-Moe had on no shirt and his skinny torso was filled with tattoos. Locking the door behind them, he waved for Nuk to follow him and they went through the back storage area through the kitchen. When they entered the smoky living room, Nuk saw two nicely dressed, fat niggas who were sitting with Xbox controllers in their hands. The game was paused and the house was silent as he came in and made eye contact.

Nuk didn't know the two fat niggas but he could see that Lil' Moe was not in the house. As far as he could see anyways.

"It's all good," G-Moe told them as he picked up a remote off the TV. "Y'all nigga be easy. This one of my brother's homies. Keep an eye out front while I take care of this business."

Once G-Moe said that, he clicked back on the stereo and the two fat niggas returned to playing Xbox. G-Moe took Nuk into a back room and closed the door behind them. He then walked past Nuk and seemed to head in the direction of his closet.

"You came just in time too cause my lil' mans was just askin' me to front him some work and I was just—" But before he could finish his sentence, Nuk sideswiped him hard in the face with the heavy steel of the gun. G-Moe let out a small, quick groan of pain as he fell and flopped on the two queen-size mattresses that were on the floor. Like on a lion on its prey, Nuk leaped onto the man's chest, covered his mouth, and started rapidly beating him about the face and head with his gun. Blood spattered and flesh split as Nuk pounded G-Moe into unconsciousness. Filled with wild adrenaline, Nuk turned back and watched the door with his gun pointed at the ready. When he assessed that the scuffle wasn't heard over the music and

TV, he scrambled to gag and hog-tie G-Moe with whatever he could find. When he was done, he readied himself to exit the room and attack. With his hand on the doorknob, he counted to himself "1… 2… 3!" before he boldly came out, walked briskly down the hall with his gun already raised, rounded the corner to the living room, and put two silent holes in the two fat niggas' chest and face. Nuk felt like he was unstoppable as he stood breathing hard with wild eyes. He then cut the music off, listened for any sounds coming from upstairs, and cautiously searched upstairs. When he found out that he was alone, he slipped on a white pair of latex gloves and ransacked the house from top to bottom searching for drugs and money.

Ten minutes after his search, he had found three ounces of heroin, three loose bundle-packs which came off the two dead men and G-Moe, a little over sixteen thousand in cash, and five handguns. Nuk didn't take the guns but he took everything else. He carefully crept back outside where he opened the backdoor to the stolen Prius. From there, he went back into the backroom where G-Moe still was out cold and wrapped him up in a bed comforter. Nuk hoisted G-Moe onto his shoulder like a floor rug, took him to the backyard, and quickly tossed him in the backseat of the car. He then simply backed out of the driveway with his body low in the seat and drove off down Everheart Street. When he felt he was a safe distance away, he got on his cell and called Juliet.

"Hello," she answered.

"Be dressed and ready when I come get you in one hour," he told her simply and hung up.

On the other side of the phone, Juliet's nerves trembled inside her. "Oh shit," she thought.

Chapter 21

"Where are we going, Willie?" Juliet asked, looking out the passenger side window.

"We here now," Nuk told her as he pulled into a large, empty parking lot. It was four o'clock in the evening and he had driven far out west to the Dan Ryan Woods forest preserve. The wooded area stretched over eleven blocks and was a place someone could get lost in. It was one of those grey skied days which made the area look eerie and creepy. Juliet didn't know what to expect as she followed behind Nuk into the tall trees. He hadn't said much of anything as far as an explanation was concerned and honestly it made her uneasy. After walking for five quiet minutes deep into the cover of the woods, Juliet could no longer see anything around her but forest.

"Hey... Come on, Nuk. What's going on?" she asked finally.

Nuk was in his madness and was zoned out replaying the deeds he had done earlier. He was just going about the motions as if he was alone, but her words snapped him back. "Shordy... we here now," he told her.

Juliet didn't see what he was talking about until he stepped to the side and she could see a large hole a few feet ahead. There were no words between them, she just clutched her purse to her chest and stepped slowly over to it. Juliet's heart began to beat double time once she looked into the rich, dark earth and saw the man bound and gagged. She didn't recognize who he was by face, but once she examined him closer and saw the tattoo on his bare stomach, she knew he was the man who raped and robbed her. The man in the hole lay on his side covered with blood on his face and dirty on his moist flesh. When he saw Juliet, he began to struggle to break free, but he didn't plead for his life. Instead, he became angry and lashed out verbally the best way he could.

"Ahhh, you 'itch! You hunky hitch! 'Uck you!" he spat at her.

Suddenly Juliet was filled with mixed emotions. She felt anger and fear. When Nuk came and joined her at her side, she flinched when he spoke.

"This what you wanted, right?" he asked her.

Juliet's throat was dry and she felt clammy. She felt slightly lightheaded but she knew she couldn't renege on what she asked for. So she cleared her throat, dug clumsily into her purse and came out with her gun.

"Hold the fuck on!" Nuk said, shocked. He grabbed her hand. "Where you get that shit?!"

"What? Mama Ree leant it to me," she told him, confused.

"Ain't dat a bitch? Gimme dis shit," Nuk said, taking the gun out of her hand. G-Moe was still ranting and squirming in the hole but drew no attention. Nuk continued. "Shordy, you a trip… here," he said, pulling his own gun and handing it to her.

"What's wrong with that one?" she asked, confused.

"We might be in the woods, but mufuckas still be hikin' and shit. My gun don't make no loud pop, see the tip?"

Juliet took a second and examined the heavy gun, then she aimed it down at G-Moe. Wild-eyed and thrashing about, G-Moe did his best to avoid getting hit, but he was stuck in her sights and knew his time had come.

Nuk watched Juliet aim with a trembling arm; he wanted to see if she had guts. "Study long, study wrong," he said.

Just as he said it, she pulled the trigger. The sound rang out low and muffled like *piff*. It cut through the air like a dart and tagged G-Moe in the right side of his hip. The wounded man groaned out loudly in agony as the bullet entered his body.

"Squeeze off! Kill that nigga!" Nuk demanded.

With a face twisted in horror, Juliet squeezed the trigger rapidly three times, and the hot bullets zipped into G-Moe's chest and eye socket. Silence fell upon the area and all that was left to be heard was the rustling of the trees and the chirping of the birds. G-Moe was dead. Juliet had executed him in cold blood. She stood with the gun still pointing down into the hole. She was clammy with wrecked nerves but she surprisingly felt fulfilled. Nuk took the gun out of her hand and placed it under his shirt into the waistband of his pants. He then picked up a shovel located behind the dirt mound and began shoveling dirt onto the dead man's body.

*   *   *

Days after the murders, things went back to the way they were. Nuk hit the streets of Chicago and the out-of-town streets. Juliet once again handed out orders made for ounces and the money kept coming in strong. By the end of April, Juliet's stomach was undeniably carrying a child, and she had put on more than ten pounds. When they finally reached their goal of two hundred grand and Juliet spoke with Romero on the phone, he was happy and proud.

Mama Ree along with Juliet contacted Romero's lawyer and told him what they had and he told them to wire the cash to him, so that's what they did. The next day, Juliet was back on a flight to the West Coast, and a half day later, she was back in Long Beach. As much as Juliet wanted to be at the front gate when her man was released, she knew she couldn't. So from the airport, she took a cab to her apartment and on the way called Romero's lawyer to see if he bonded him out. Mr. Blackside informed her that he would bond him out first thing in the morning. Juliet was disappointed but was also happy that when she went to sleep and woke, her man would be on his way home.

Carrying her heavy luggage in both hands from the elevator to her door was exhausting and Juliet set them down happily as she took her key out and went to unlock the door. When she did, she found the house dark and quiet. She came inside, clicked on the hallway light and came into the dark living room. She stood for a moment just happy to be back in her home and took a deep breath. From there, she headed to her bedroom and pushed the door open. When she did, she gasped in shock and clutched her chest and stomach. The room was decorated with red and pink rose petals that scattered the floor. Scented candles burned low with an aroma reminiscent of apple pie. The king-size bed had a makeover; it was now covered in red silk sheets with pillows to match. The rose petals were scattered there as well.

And standing in the corner with a large box of assorted chocolates was Romero. He was smiling warmly, dressed in nothing at all. When Juliet laid eyes on him, her heart skipped a beat and she couldn't control her emotions and just covered her face and began to cry. Romero came to her and she embraced him tightly around his neck. Romero hugged her back and was equally happy to see his number-one queen.

"You tricked me," she cried into his neck.

"I know," he chuckled. "I wanted to surprise you."

Coming apart but still in each other's arms, the reunited couple began to kiss each other deep and long.

"Babe… you're naked." She smiled, stating the obvious.

"I know, a nigga been working out every day tryna put together a bedroom body. Look at you though, you got big," he said lightly, rubbing on her stomach.

"Mhmm, and my back and feet be hurtin' and everything, babe."

"Oh yeah... well, we gon' have to make you feel better."

"We who?" She smiled as he wiped her tears away.

"Me and Lil' King," he told her, referencing to his penis. "Come on... let's take a bath."

The lovebirds bathed together in a warm bubble bath surrounded by more scented candles. Juliet sat between Romero's legs while he washed and massaged her back and neck. They spoke gently to one another about all things past, present, and future, and when they were done, they commemorated their rejoining by making sweet love on their bed of silken sheets and rose petals.

     *   *   *

Over the next five months that came, things drastically changed for Romero and Juliet. The large cash flow brought in from their previous business was gone and they could no longer afford to live in their swanky top-floor apartment, so they had to move to another place which was smaller but still nice. Nuk had sent them forty grand which was left over from the kilo and they used it as down-payment on a new way of living. Romero's court case showed no sign of slowing down. His lawyer, Peter Blackside, had put his best foot forward. He had bits of his case tossed out, motions were filed, court dates were pushed back time and time again... but in the end, the DA's office wanted either of two things. Number one being a conviction through the jury process, or number two, a harsh plea agreement.

Any way it went, Romero was looking at major prison time. Mr. Blackside told Romero that if they proceeded to trial that he felt that the overwhelming circumstantial evidence against him might be just what the jury needs to find him guilty. All Romero had in his favor was the fact that there was no actual proof that he killed or had anything to do with the victim's actual death. Mr. Blackside told Romero that he could ask for one more month-long continuance so he could make his decision, and whatever he decided, he would go to bat for him one hundred percent.

On September 14th, 2014, Juliet gave birth to a beautiful baby girl who they named Eastern Star Hinton. She was a ball of joy and the new reason for living in Romero's eyes. While Romero was incarcerated in the county jail, he had lots of free time on his hands and he finished writing his book and even began another about his life. Through the self-publishing site CreateSpace, he published his first novel and within a month's time, he had sold over 325 copies. Even though five grand was peanuts compared to what he was pulling in before… it was an honest and legit living.

*   *   *

"Ms. Witmore, how may I be of service to you?" Mr. Blackside asked, taking a seat on the corner of his desk. Juliet had made the unexpected journey down to the private practice to speak to the lawyer about something that had been on her mind for many months. She hadn't told Romero of her visit and wanted to keep it under wraps until she figured out what she could do.

"Thank you for seeing me on such short notice. Umm… concerning my boyfriend's case—"

"I'm sorry but I can't discuss details—"

"No it's not like that," she assured him. "What if someone was to come forward and admit to the charges… hypothetically speaking?"

Mr. Blackside frowned. He was puzzled at first but it took him only moment to realize what she was actually saying. "Well, hypothetically… naturally the person originally charged would be released. That is if the DA's office believed the person who came forward."

"Mm, I see… and what would the charges be for that said person?" she asked.

"Well, that would depend on what that said person was actually admitting to," he answered.

"Self-defense," she told him.

"Self-defense? Well, in this particular case… with the victim's body being moved? Could be tough to prove, but anything is possible. There can also be a lot of factors that could or could not help in that said person's favor."

There came a long pause between them, more so on Juliet's part because she was in deep contemplation. She wanted to be her man's savior once again. Juliet knew how the world worked when it came down to equality and racial fairness. Romero was a black man from Chicago who was charged with killing a white man, but Juliet was a young white female from Idaho who would be claiming self-defense from a potential rapist.

"Ms. Witmore," Mr. Blackside called to her. "Is everything all right? Is there something you want me to know?"

Juliet swallowed saliva. "I think I'm going to need some representation, Mr. Blackside," she told him.

"Well, you've come to the right place. I know a good attorney who'll take care of you. Now, Ms. Witmore, just to be clear. What will you be needing representation for?"

"A confession to a death, but from self-defense."

Mr. Blackside reached over on his desk and pushed his intercom for his secretary.

"Brenda?"

"Yes, Mr. Blackside," the female voice answered.

"Get me Sam Rosenbaum's number, and also deliver Jim Gorden to me from the paralegal department. Tell him to prepare to draw up an affidavit, please."

"Right away, sir," the secretary told him.

"Are you sure you wanna go through with this, Ms. Witmore?" he asked her as he stood up and sat down in his chair.

"As sure as I'll ever be," she told him, heavyhearted.

* * *

When Juliet returned home, all she wanted to do was hold her baby girl in her arms. When she came through the front door, Romero was in the living room sitting on the edge of the couch. He had already been contacted by his lawyer and informed of what had taken place. He was highly upset but strangely flattered. Juliet saw the look on his face and knew he knew, but she proceeded to the baby's room. When Romero entered the room shortly behind her, he found Juliet cuddling the small child in her arms while the child slept. He paused at the door for a moment just watching them, then he came over to them.

"Who the hell told you to do what you did, Juliet?" Romero asked her sternly, but in a low tone.

Juliet cooed the slumbering baby and rubbed its back softly. She had been dreading confronting Romero but now she had no choice. "Do you love me, Romero?" she asked simply.

"What? Of course, but what that got to—"

"Good," she cut in. "Because I've loved you since that first night you fed me McDonalds. Please never question why I do the things I do for you. Just know that I do them for you because it's my desire to. You can't beat that case and you know it, and you can't go back to jail and leave me out here alone. Not with this child."

"Hold on, I said—"

"Romero, please," she interjected strongly. "Let me speak for a change."

He sighed. "Go 'head," he told her.

"Baby… You are the king, the head of this family, but what's a family without its head? You have so much going for you now. Your books doing well and you're making local appearances for signings and things. Now you'll be having another book out soon and there's no doubt in my mind that it'll be twice as popular. Baby I need you out here. Your daughter needs you out here."

Romero took in what she said to him and it touched his heart to hear it. Juliet was right about everything she said. Romero knew that if he went away, it would be for a while, and even though he knew she was loyal, he also knew she wasn't prepared to take on so much responsibility alone. Romero had visions of her turning tricks to pay the rent and risking her own freedom to get money to support not only herself and his child, but him as well. He saw visions of her moving to Chicago and moving in with his mother, living off public assistance and becoming a victim of the ghetto. Romero couldn't have that, not for Juliet and not for his daughter.

Romero was torn and confused. He took a seat on the rocking chair that he bought to rock the baby in. He placed his hands on his face in aggravation. Juliet came over to him and carefully got down on both knees before him, then with her free hand, she pulled one of his hands down and held it. Romero looked at her and could no longer be upset. He looked to his daughter's round head and touched her fine, dark hair.

"Make me your wife, Romero," Juliet said to him.

There was a pause between them as they looked into each other's eyes. Romero was surprised to hear her ask him that because it was his plan to do so once he released his second book.

"Stand up for me," he asked her.

When Juliet stood, Romero went down on one knee before her and took her hand. "This love that we have comes only once in a lifetime. Some people even go their whole lives without finding it, but you... and me... from the very start were meant to be together. You're the perfect woman for me, and the perfect example of a woman for our daughter. I got nothing but love for you, Juliet Witmore, and I would be honored if you would accept me as your soul mate, king, lover, best friend... and husband."

By the end of Romero's speech, Juliet was in tears. She nodded her head yes and Romero kissed her hand and rose up and embraced her.

Epilogue

When Peter Blackside presented the signed affidavit of Juliet Witmore's confession, they dropped the charges against Romero and demanded she turn herself in. Romero was off the hook for murder, but the DA held fast on the charge of intimidation of an informant, and he was hit with four years probation without jail time. Juliet on the other hand, was hit with second-degree murder. In the end, her lawyer, Sam Rosenbaum, got her a plea deal of five years, and since she spend six months in the county jail, she was credited for that time served. Juliet had never been in major trouble with the law before, so she was also eligible for any good conduct credits that the prison may have offered. With any luck and her good behavior, she would parole out in less than five.

Romero's autobiography "Twisted Life" hit the internet was a major success in the self-publishing world. He sold 932 copies in his first month and was offered a publishing contract with a large firm. As savvy as he was, Romero turned the offer down but managed to ink a distribution deal which placed both his books in many bookstores across the U.S.

Romero and Juliet sealed their vows of love legally while she was incarcerated and a couple of months later, they consummated their union sexually on a weekend-long conjugal visit. Even though Romero was out on his own with a child, he had plenty of support from his family back home. Sometimes he would fly his mother out to watch the baby for a few days while he visited with his wife and sometimes he himself would fly back home for a weekend.

Romero located Jennybell's family and sent them a small package. Inside the package was a signed copy of his autobiography, many photos of Jennybell and the rest of the family when she was with him, two thousand dollars, and a letter.

One afternoon while Romero was speaking about his book at a Barnes & Noble, he thought he saw Sandra in the back of the audience. When he shaded his eyes to see more clearly, the female had turned and left.

Life for Romero's small family was a work in progress but he was up to the task. Juliet sat and did her time without complaint. She called home twice a week, wrote home three times a month, went to school, got visits, and was financially stable. She loved her husband and couldn't wait to rejoin him and their daughter… once she was free.

www.ingramcontent.com/pod-product-compliance
Lightning Source LLC
Chambersburg PA
CBHW022108280326
41933CB00007B/307